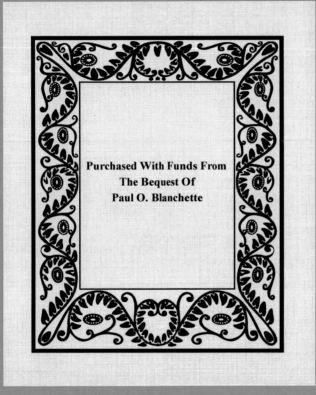

BIRTH, DEATH, AND A TRACTOR

BIRTH, DEATH, AND A TRACTOR

Connecting An Old
Farm To a New Family

KELLY PAYSON-ROOPCHAND

Down East Books

CAMDEN, MAINE

Published by Down East Books
A wholly owned subsidary of The Rowman & Littlefield Publishing Group, Inc.
4501 Forbes Boulevard, Suite 200, Lanham, Maryland 20706
www.rowman.com

Unit A, Whitacre Mews, 26-34 Stannary Street, London SE11 4AB

Distributed by NATIONAL BOOK NETWORK

British Library Cataloguing in Publication Information Available

Library of Congress Cataloging-in-Publication Data
Payson-Roopchand, Kelly.
  Birth, death, and a tractor : connecting an old farm to a new family / Kelly
Payson-Roopchand.
    pages cm
  ISBN 978-1-60893-411-9 (cloth : alk. paper) — ISBN 978-1-60893-412-6
(electronic) 1. Farm life—Maine—Somerville—History. 2. Family farms—Maine—
Somerville—History. 3. Payson-Roopchand, Kelly. I. Title.
  S521.5.M2P39 2015
  630.9741'57—dc23   2015006018

∞™ The paper used in this publication meets the minimum requirements of American
National Standard for Information Sciences—Permanence of Paper for Printed Library
Materials, ANSI/NISO Z39.48-1992.

Printed in the United States of America

In memory of Beth Ann Eisen,
in whose studio I started this book,
and in whose generous spirit I learned to let mine sing.

Contents

PART III: SPRING
Weaving the Cloth

PART IV: SUMMER
The Possibilities of Ripeness

Acknowledgments

This story owes its inspiration and its humanity to the warm and generous spirits of Don and Shirley Hewett, who embody the best of the small-farm family. Thank you for welcoming us to the farm and sharing your stories. Thanks, likewise, to the younger generation of Hewetts, who have trusted me to recount a part of their family's history.

This book owes its existence to my parents, Stephanie and Smoky Payson, who have supported its creation in every way possible. Thank you for helping us keep body and soul together during the long years it took me to finish the book.

To our pumpkin vine of family and friends, who enrich our lives—and sometimes appear in my stories!—a huge thank you for bringing your own unique flavors to our farm. A garden is richer for diversity!

During the research phases of the book, I developed a deep gratitude for the staff members of libraries and archives throughout the world. I would particularly like to thank the staff of the Maine State Library, the Maine State Archives, and the Maine State Museum, as well as the Maine State Law and Legislative Library and the Maine Department of Transportation Library. The clerks at the Lincoln County Registry of Deeds helped me to locate and copy important early deeds, especially the missing survey of 1818, which required the ever-patient clerks to keep looking, one more time . . .

I am grateful for the enthusiastic assistance of those who helped me preserve important historic documents. John Goodine, at Elm City Photo, took on the huge project of scanning the historic photos of the farm, occasionally bringing them back from obscurity. Kathryn Gaynor used her professional skills to transcribe the tantalizing but (for me) unreadable letter of Samuel Kennedy, from 1830.

I, and all my readers, owe a huge thanks to my dear friend, Joanie Dean, who showed me how to weave all of the different stories together without too many tangles. I also give thanks to (and for) Jennifer Caven, who as a professional editor, reassured me that I did *not* need to rewrite the beginning, giving it instead a meticulous copyedit and helping me to submit that query letter!

On a personal level, I need to thank Deanne Hermann, who left us too soon, but not before she made it clear that Maine is the *best* place to farm. For Beth, there is no adequate way to say thank you; yours is a gift of the spirit. Special thanks to the exceptionally talented photographer Audra Medunitza, who let me use her beautiful photo of Beth.

Finally, I need to say thanks to my sweet children, Sarita and Keiran Roopchand, and my most beloved husband, Anil. I do it for you, and, in great joy, with you. I most certainly could not have done it without you! Thank you.

AUTHOR'S NOTE

THE WORLD you are about to enter is both real and imagined. Like any story of the past it is, in part, just that—a story. Although the details of human lives can be found in names and dates, it is the quieter thing, the soft spirit of human longing, that eludes us when we try to pin the past down, wiggling, onto the page. Yet it is these emotions that bring the past to life, and let us suddenly stand beside these bygone farmers as welcome visitors to their world. So I have dared to imagine their feelings at events we all can recognize, to wonder at beginnings and to grieve at loss.

The facts of their lives, no less exciting—and at times more surprising—have been gathered from many sources, both general and specific. The family's oral history was shared over many cozy evenings and repeated enough times to be its own verification. Old photo albums and recipe books were passed, crackling, from hand to hand, while treasured letters were carefully lifted from weightless envelopes, their paper as thin as an old woman's skin.

To understand the farm's place within the changing world, I turned to history books of Somerville and Maine, New England, and the nation. In particular, I relied heavily on the detailed works of Clarence Day for the specifics of early colonial agriculture in Maine, as well as the brilliantly annotated photo books of William Bunting, which put the faces of the past—literally—in front of you.

I was able to search early censuses from my second-floor office by tapping the deep wells of the Internet, particularly the formidable collections of ancestry.com. Verifying the farm's origins required a more tactile involvement, from archives to county deed offices, aided by invariably helpful librarians. Archives staff helped me to discover the contentious land-settlement history of central Maine, which, as I tracked it more closely, revolved around our very farm.

Although the town's early vital records were lost in a fire in 1940, the discovery of a missing survey in the Lincoln County Registry of Deeds' office gave me an amazing view of the earliest settlements. Where legal records have conflicted with family genealogies, I have relied on the official record, with apologies to the scribes of the past.

Some things I still do not (and may never) know, for the holes of the past are large indeed, and my own time more limited than their scope. I am not a historian, but a farmer, and, at best, a slow writer. Like the reader, I learned the farm's history as I went along, delving into historical accounts. However, if this book was ever to be written, I had at some point to stop my research and set the story down, accepting its imperfections. Therefore, for what I have omitted and for any mistakes I've made, I ask forgiveness—and correction—as I feel nothing but respect for those who have walked before me.

ONE FARM, SIX GENERATIONS
YEARS OF OPERATION
TYPE OF FARM

Lydia Brown – Sebra Crooker
1808-1850s
Homestead

Julia Crooker – Ephraim Kennedy
1829-1891
Homestead

Calista Chadwick – Francis Kennedy
1860-1916
Sheep

Edith Kennedy – William Hewett
1892-1946
Poultry and Dairy

Jane Nutting – Lloyd Hewett
1918-1958
Dairy

Shirley Brown – Don Hewett
1936-1986
Dairy ·

PART I

FALL:
BEGINNING AT
THE END

THE STORY

WHAT NEEDS to be told? There was a beginning and a middle to the story—indeed, ever so many middles—woven across the rippling of years. An ending? Perhaps. Yes, perhaps, for many such stories have already come to a close. But does it need to end? Or could we—should we—keep the story alive?

Maybe you can decide, for it is your story, too.

THE ROAD

THERE IS a dirt road, comfortable in its existence, familiar with the fields it cuts through. It has been a dirt road for as long as it can remember, since the first European settlers cut a track through the forest. It has known the slow determination of feet, the imperturbable plod of oxen, and the lighter dance of horses' hooves, and it bears now the rolling speed of our thousand desires.

It is a quiet road—so quiet that you can still hear the land, singing or sighing or howling. Our voices cut across the silence briefly, raised in the urgency of our short span of years. There is the occasional engine, the purposeful hum of the tractor, or the passing rumble of car tires on gravel, propelling our busy lives. But it is the sound of the land that remains when they die away, singing through a thousand throats, beast and bird, tree and grass, brook and wind. Accustomed as we are to the drowning noise of technology, it is a strangely quiet song, and our senses stretch outward, aware.

For six generations, the story has woven itself into this land, each chapter beginning—and ending—on the road. Now I too follow its quiet path, joining my life with the land, adding my story to its rippling fabric. Five generations chose to stay here, but I, like the first generation, had to find my own way home . . .

1976

ENCHANTMENT

WHEN I was six, my family moved to a small island in Maine, a child's land of enchantment, with pebble beaches and stone ledges. We came in the fall, when all the summer houses had been boarded up, and we seemed to be the only family on the ridge.

I do not remember how I found the small sheep farm—whether I pushed through the overgrown path myself, or whether my older brothers led the way in some pirate adventure. Regardless, I was welcomed as naturally as an errant grandchild, and for three years the farm became the center of my world. Every afternoon, when the school bus released me to my own navigation, I would run first to the farm, hoping to be in time for chores.

For a brief moment each day, I was a farm girl, in a world that was—fantastically—both magical and real. There I had no need of unicorns, for springtime brought lambs, sliding wet onto the straw, glistening with newness. A few, rejected by their mothers, became mine, and they cried as eagerly as children when they heard my voice. Sucking lustily at their bottles, their unexpectedly long tails wiggled constantly, a moving exclamation of delight.

5

When hens refused to surrender their nests, I learned to slip my hand under their soft breasts, feeling for the eggs' smooth warmth against the bristling hay. Come fall, I dug for the first time in a garden, amazed to see potatoes rising out of the earth like buried treasure. When a determined sheep joined us in the garden, I wrote my own story of escape and capture, carefully illustrating each of its errant footprints.

A few years later we moved inland, and I mourned the loss of the farm, my days suddenly empty. With my mother as chief conspirator, we decided to start our own farm. Taking advantage of my more prudent father's brief absence, we quickly renovated an old shed, painting it a cheery yellow to match our house. My farmer friends, awaiting our call, drove from the coast with one of my bottle babies—now a bossy young ewe—and ten laying hens. By the time my father returned, our home had become a farm, and my sheep, aptly named Special K, was supreme commander.

Although we were unprepared and inefficient, the animals taught us much, and, by the time I went to college, I was no longer satisfied with the usual pursuits of academia and the inevitable progression from classroom to office. In 1988 I dropped out of Harvard, seeking answers I couldn't find in the hallowed stacks of Widener Library.

When I told my dismayed parents that I was pursuing the meaning of life instead of my bachelor's degree, their enthusiasm was somewhat less than I expected. However, passionate and pigheaded, I wandered and questioned for several years, trying different jobs, different schools, always seeking meaning.

Finally, when an exchange program led me to a small island in the Caribbean, I was drawn back to my childhood passion. Visiting farmer friends, I would lend a hand as they prepared their day's meal, talking and laughing as we worked. Sitting on the back step, we shelled endless piles of pigeon peas, separating the rattling brown pods from the sticky green as their children ran and shouted in the yard around us.

Some days we dug cassava; other days we harvested the thin-skinned tropical pumpkin or cut callaloo, the sweetly succulent island amaranth. I learned to make coconut milk, rubbing the hard, white flesh against a homemade grater, its tin surface perforated with nail holes. Later, squeezing the flaked coconut in a water bath, I marveled at the creamy milk that sprang forth, obscuring my hands.

To my northern eyes, their garden seemed unlikely, a few scattered bushes and trees without apparent rows or borders. Yet every afternoon, they picked or dug up or knocked down the rewards of their garden, and slowly, carefully, transformed them into a meal. As their children clustered eagerly around the pot, there seemed little separation between the nourishment of earth and child.

Sharing in their meal, I felt my restlessness subside. I had no reason to leave, nothing left to seek. Here was a life which had always spoken to me, which had drawn me in before I had questions, but only knew, naturally, my center of gravity. Keenly, then, I felt a longing for my own plot of earth, my own relationship with soil and sky.

And so I became a student of agriculture, and while my parents celebrated my return to academia, I was surprised to find myself studying chemistry and physics, economics and ecology. Always it seemed as if the farm was just one step away, and so I continued through a master's degree and a doctorate. But the more I studied, the farther I was directed away from the land. Agricultural students were not groomed to be farmers, but policy makers or researchers, shaping agriculture's future.

Pursuing my doctoral degree, I returned to the Caribbean and other people's farms. This time, my dreams resurfaced in unexpected form. When I met Anil, he was working in the department of agriculture at the university in Trinidad, and I did not imagine that our connection would stray from the agricultural and academic.

Like me, Anil had always longed for a farm. Although his family no longer kept animals, farming was part of his heritage, and stories of bossy cows and dangerous bulls had filled his childhood. Not one to be easily thwarted, he tied together some sturdy glass bottles to serve as his herd. Every morning he tethered his bottle cows on a lush patch of grass, and every afternoon he moved them into the shade.

Boyhood did not end Anil's fascination, nor young manhood overwhelm it with the imperatives of adult life. While Trinidad as a nation placed her faith in industrialization, Anil left high school with an unwavering interest in agriculture.

In 1995 he found his way to the Eastern Caribbean Institute of Agriculture and Forestry (ECIAF). Unlike most American agricultural schools, ECIAF emphasized the practical as well as the theoretical, and Anil plunged gladly into the realities of farm life, absorbing the skills he had longed for. Every morning he headed to field or barn, ready to get his hands dirty. If one day he extracted honey, the next he would graft citrus or slaughter chickens. At exam time, he stood before piles of seeds, sorting and identifying.

Two years later, Anil graduated with an award for excellence in farm practicals. Known by his peers as the "human milking machine," he was, indisputably, the fastest milker on campus, a distinction not easily earned on the restless Xibu-cross cattle.

Experience only increased Anil's interest in farming, and he continued his studies at the University of the West Indies. By the time I met him, he had finished his master's in animal science and was planning a PhD. I was just starting my dissertation research, and we quickly connected on matters agricultural and academic.

Despite our professional intentions, we grew closer, and our relationship balanced on the edge of our deepening friendship, swaying. I tried to resist, reluctant to form a long-distance relationship. But here, finally, was a man who understood, in a personal way, the passion of the land. Here, for him, was a woman who recognized the wealth of his soul, who saw value in the natural and wild.

We gave in and spoke of love and family, trying to reconcile careers and countries, but as yet we dreamed little of farming, two professionals trained away from the very soil we studied. We were to be advisors, researchers, policy makers. We were to impact farmers, but not to be farmers. The bias was subtle but ever-present, and it bound our dreams to academic conventions.

When marriage interrupted my academic progress, we moved into my parents' house in Maine so I could finish my dissertation. Anil began to explore my parents' land, spending hours in the woods, cutting firewood, clearing land. Their property had once been a farm, and the remains of those times were all around, slowly surrendering to forest and age. The once-imposing barn sagged like a work-worn horse, and the turkey sheds housed raccoons and woodchucks.

In the evenings we visited friends and talked of the many new farms that were emerging from overgrown fields, and the increasing number of local farmers' markets. Gathered around the table, we sampled our friends' homemade cheeses and heirloom tomatoes and wondered what we had eaten all our life.

These new farmers were passionate, committed, and—for the most part—untrained in agriculture. Looking at each other across the table, we could see the same thought in each other's eyes: *If they could do this on conviction alone, couldn't we also, after all our years of agricultural study?* As we drove home, we would put our academic training to work, analyzing their production systems and the emerging market opportunities for small, artisanal farms.

That spring, battling with the final drafts of my dissertation, we started to talk about life after graduation. We had assumed I would get a job in agricultural policy, most likely ending up in a large, metropolitan area, and Anil would start his PhD. Sitting on the porch, watching night settle over the trees and fields, it was hard to imagine life in the city, bound by concrete and steel, the uncompromising angles of urban life replacing the delicate fluidity of the countryside.

It was even more difficult to consign myself to a lifetime of work one step removed from the farm. I asked Anil about his goals and objectives, and we talked about careers and children and happiness. Finally, we admitted that we wanted to stay in the country—that we had always dreamed of farming. Didn't we now have the skills, even if we lacked the capital?

We were at first embarrassed to admit our dream, as if we were betraying our training. Everybody knew that farmers worked themselves to the bone but made no money. Yet why, oh why, if the rewards were so small, the work so unstimulating, did generations of farmers persist, even when there were other options? Why did they continue to lead small lives, tied to a piece of land with purse strings forever tight, bone-tired in the evening and often still weary in the morning? Nobody seemed to know—or had they forgotten?—the joys of working the land, of life bounded only by the sky, of piling plates with food they had harvested. Perhaps farmers did not need as much money to feed their hungry souls; perhaps the work itself was fulfilling, and a tired body felt good at the end of the day.

As for the perceived lack of intellectual stimulation, I knew that farming was far from simple work. A student of agricultural science, I had delved into the mysteries of life and growth, both plant and animal. I had traced the intricate cycles of soil and water and many times, deep in a textbook, had stopped reading, amazed and gratified by the intricate beauty of the natural world.

It was amazing that life worked at all, but it did, and beautifully, following a dance of such precision that it seemed unwise to insert oneself. Yet cut in we did, with clumsy feet, leading our partner into our own rhythms, demanding new steps. To be a farmer was a bold act, requiring skill and confidence to match our partner and call forth her best. What greater joy could there be than to dance with the natural world?

And so we admitted our dreams and laughed with relief to find our buried hopes as treasure in each other's eyes. As the darkness deepened, we lingered outside, making plans both probable and improbable. Armed with the arsenal of agricultural knowledge that we had paid for with years of confinement, we were free to be hopeful children again, filled with optimism and joy. Surely there was a farm in our future . . .

SEPTEMBER 2009
THE END OF THE ROAD

IT IS morning, and I come downstairs, one-year-old Keiran riding on my hip. Already impatient to be outside, he wiggles as I put on his shoes. He is almost independent, needing my hand for balance but otherwise impatiently tugging, a fish desperate to escape the line. As we step over the threshold, he pauses, his hand quiet in mine, looking around at the day. Like all good farmers, he starts each day by taking stock . . .

Nestled in a bowl of trees, our farm is a breathtaking remnant of a six-generation family farm, connected to the outside world by a mile of dirt road. Old apple trees line the road, their branches as twisted and forlorn as the tumbled stone walls below, yet each spring they coax forth an abundance of flowers, and each fall they make a brave offering of nameless apples. Most are small and sour, probably cider apples, but to my son they are a treasure for the picking. "Ap, ap," he entreats, pulling me toward the tempting fruit. I hoist him into the tree, supporting him with my belly, once again swelling with new life.

Successful in his quest, Keiran holds an apple aloft, then points to the goat pen where Manley, our Nubian buck, is pacing in anticipation. A big

11

goat, Manley's head is level with mine when he jumps onto the gate, and caution tempers Keiran's excitement as he holds the apple out. Straining forward, Manley mouths the entire apple, trying to find an entry into its smooth slickness.

While Keiran admires Manley, I watch the female goats, safely separated from their ardent suitor. Aligned along the barn ramp, the does bask in the morning sun, their coats shining: the multicolored Nubians with their roman noses and floppy ears, and the glistening white Saanens, their noses dished and ears erect. Heedless of the wet grass soaking his soft leather shoes, Keiran toddles to the rail to inspect the herd. Pulling himself up on tiptoe, he peers over the rail, resting his cheek on the graying board. Together we are quiet, humans and goats, enjoying the view.

Our house and barn lie partway down a hill, our fields sloping gently to a brook. Once a seasonal stream, the brook has widened below our house into a broad marsh, the work of the resident beavers. This morning the marsh is partially obscured by a low fog that rests along the length of the brook, heralding the change of season. The rising sun, angling down to the river, lights the fog from within, slowly melting . . .

The sound of a vehicle approaching, its tires crunching over the gravel, draws our attention back to the road. With only two other houses before the road ends, a passing car is a notable event. We wave as a truck comes into view, and the neighbors wave back as they pass. Here at the end of the road, we know each other's news—not in the modern sense of gossip, but in the way of community, where each of our small stories is shared and important.

An airplane drones above us, and Keiran leans back in my arms, searching for the contrail. He is fascinated with all things motorized and lifts his hand in imitation of the plane. Every morning a plane passes about this time, flying low, easily visible. High above, a few others pass silently, their faint, smoky trails soon blown apart. This is our traffic.

Our road is named Hewett Road for the family that farmed this land for six generations, and our farm is named Pumpkin Vine Family Farm for the family ties that stretch, vine-like, around the globe.[1]

Grounded in the land, the farm connects us through time and space, drawing us irresistibly home.

Don and Shirley Hewett, the last of their family to farm this land, now live across the road in a small house overlooking the fields. Like the generations before him, Don had poured his life, body and soul, into the farm. A tall man, bending now before age's advance, he has a strong and steady presence, as reassuring and timeless as the land itself. Just as clearly as he shaped the land, plowing the fields with horses and, later, tractors, so the farm has marked him, in the strength of his large hands and the quiet contentment of his spirit.

But Don himself had no farmer heir, and as the years passed, he had been forced to sell first his cows and then his farm. He had built himself a new house on the hilltop, where he watched the barn and fields slowly fill with the clutter of neglect. Then we arrived, and shortly thereafter, our son Keiran, and new life crept into the farm, small but irresistible, like the trickle of ice melting in the spring.

Like Don, Keiran was born on this farm, and he belonged to the land in a way that I never would, much as I loved it. The land called to him, and he answered without restraint, eager to know goat and river, sky and apple tree. Walking the road in his yellow boots, he seemed a small sprite, a laughing piece of the farm itself, joyful in its million transformations. He gravitated toward Don as naturally as the young colt shadows the stallion, mimicking his behavior. Watching Don astride his tractor, Keiran trembled with longing, waiting his turn at the helm.

Yet small farms such as ours faced an uncertain future, and there was no guarantee that Keiran's beloved world would survive. For more than two hundred years, our farm had been sustained by love and necessity, but much had changed since the first seeds had sprouted, hesitantly raising their leaves among the stumps of a forest clearing. Nowadays mega-farms flood grocery stores with cheap food, and small farms are considered a hobby, too expensive to maintain. We are committed and stubborn, yet reality still stares us in the face, coldly uncompromising, waiting for us to admit our mistake.

But seeing Don and Keiran together, it was hard for me to believe we'd made a mistake—that it was not, in fact, deeply right. Don was one of those people we all longed to meet, if not to be, and at eighty-seven years old his gentle spirit sparkled with a delight and mischief equal to Keiran's own. It seemed a rare gift to grow up on a farm and work the land, to know deeply and immediately one's place in the cycle of life.

Despite our vastly different backgrounds, Don and Shirley had welcomed us as farmers, gladly sharing their family's story. Shirley was as warm and chatty as the most beloved of grandmothers, and, in the homey comfort of their living room, their stories flowed freely.

Together we pored over old photographs, curious to see the farm, so familiar and yet so strange, other families gathered on the porch, looking out at us. As we turned the brittle pages of a handwritten cookbook, we lingered over the recipes, laughing at the personal comments and wondering what *our* children would think of "Crybaby Cookies." Every day, as we worked to revive the farm, we felt their presence supporting us.

Their family's imprint on the farm was clear, from the hand-hewn timbers rising to the hayloft, each ax stroke clearly visible, to the sloping fields, cleared first with oxen and then with horses. Conscious of generations of love and labor, we fought to grow our little farm, struggling with the constraints of modern life.

It was a financial stretch, requiring both of our incomes to pay the bills, and I wondered how we would find time to farm. When I despaired, Anil reminded me, "You do not find such a place and let it go." And so we farmed on evenings and weekends, working outside until night blinded us, the farm always our joy and our goal.

As much as we had longed for this life, we had not imagined the depth of our delight in the experience. The farm gave us immediate connection, the vitality of beauty and pain in the smallest of chores, as well as deep reflection when we paused, elbows scraped and dirty, to consider the significance of our acts.

With blood and dirt commingled on our hands, we understood the perspective of the pig and the potato. We were sowers and reapers, standing at the two ends of life. As we shaped lives, so also were we shaped, as we ate and worked and faded away, our edges slowly dimming. Hearing the stories of previous generations, I saw our own lives reflected, and understood that we too were just a passing moment, a short slide from birth to death.

The more we lived the farm life, the less we could imagine any other. As we milked the does or weeded the garden, our off-farm jobs seemed insubstantial, the shadows of clouds quickly passing over the solid reality of our fields. This was the only work that felt alive and whole, and we longed to stay here, to pour the skill and labor of our hands into this land.

Nor were we alone in our longings. Every day, splashed across the newspapers like tales of forbidden love, I read of people seeking reconnection to food and farms. In our rush toward comfort and convenience, we had not fully appreciated how much we had left behind. Along with the sweat and dirt of farm work came a bone-deep satisfaction from our connection to the land. Computer games and reality TV could not replace the direct participation in life and death that small farms offered.

Having divorced itself from a land-based lifestyle, society needed to find new ways to relate to small farms, not only as consumers but as participants. Our greatest need, it seemed, was not the physical nourishment of our bodies, but the peace and connection of our spirits. Beyond fresh local food, we needed the *experience* of farming.

As Richard Louv reminds us, "for today's young people, the familial and cultural linkage to farming is disappearing . . ." In 2012, farms comprised only 1.8 percent of US households, down from 40 percent in 1900, and few children ever set foot on a small farm, much less have a meaningful long-term relationship with one.[2]

This, then, is the story of our farm, but also of the choices we make as a society. As we follow the six generations who shaped this farm, it reminds us of who we have been and, as we struggle to revive the farm, it challenges us to choose who we will become.

Do we value a sense of connection, a deeper understanding of our own place in the cycles of life? Will we make space for small farms in the future and find meaningful ways to reconnect our children—and ourselves—with them?

Here at the end of the road, we have found a peace and vitality that connect us deeply—to each other, to the land, and to its generations of farmers. They have also passed along this road, women and men who dreamed and worked, loved and mourned and passed on, leaving this farm to nurture their children. Now it is my children who run, laughing, in yellow boots, and I who am the farmer, the dreamer, and the storyteller.

Listen, then, before the stories whisper into silence. Listen, and I will tell you tales of the farm—stories of birth, death, and a tractor.

NOTES

1. *Pumpkin vine family* is a Trinidadian expression referring to large extended-family networks.

2. Richard Louv, *Last Child in the Woods* (Chapel Hill, NC: Algonquin Books, 2008), p. 19. Farm data from 2012 was updated using the 2010 federal population census of 116.7 million households, and the 2012 agricultural census of 2.1 million farm households.

1808^1

SEBRA AND LYDIA CROOKER

THE ROAD is not yet a road, but voices approach along it, defining its future path. Once there were other voices that came and went with the seasons, but they are quiet now, and the valleys listen in vain for their arrival. Now, everywhere, there are new voices, speaking a different language, and the hills echo with their persistent labors.[2]

The forest here is thick with maple and oak, ash and birch, and the trees yield reluctantly to the passage of an oxcart,[3] laden with life and intent. A man, Sebra Crooker, thirty-eight years old, walks at the ox's head, guiding it along a narrow track. The path is more promise than passage, and the branches, disturbed, slap at the ox's flanks, but the beast plods steadily on. Only the man raises his hand, pushing back the trees.

Walking beside the two-wheeled cart, his wife Lydia, thirty-seven, keeps an eye on their daughters, Mary, two, and Mercy, four, who have fallen asleep in the cart. They had left Newcastle before dawn that morning and walked through midday, shielded from the heat by the overhanging branches. Now the sun is descending again, and still they walk on, trusting Sebra's guidance.

That morning, the boys, eight-year-old Sebra Jr. and seven-year-old William, had run ahead, pushing their livestock—a cow, a pig, and two sheep—in front of the cart. But it was a long walk—some twenty miles, Sebra had told her—and the boys had lagged as the day wore on. Luckily, the ox was slow,[4] and young Lydia, a capable eleven, had taken over when they tired. Watching her eldest daughter's back leading them into the trees, Lydia sighs, reminded of the reason for this never-ending march.

She had been happy in Newcastle, happier than she had ever expected when she stood on the dock in Plymouth ten years ago, waiting for the boat that would carry her north.[5] True, Pembroke was crowded, Marshfield was crowded—indeed, all of Plymouth County was crowded—and food had seemed as scarce as firewood some days,[6] but she knew nothing of frontier life, and she had wondered how she would manage.

To her surprise, Newcastle had turned out to be a bustling—if somewhat rough—seaport, and Sebra had plenty of work as a shipwright. He had bought a good piece of land, and Lydia had soon settled into her new life, busy with the demands of a homestead and children. But Sebra had remained restless, buying and selling land up and down the Maine coast,[7] as if goaded by opportunity.

Then the rumors had begun—of land just up the river that was free for the taking. The land, they said, had been granted to British noblemen by King George, but surely the deeds of past monarchs were of no consequence in their new country. They had fought—and won!—a war for independence, and now it was up to them to make their own future.[8]

A year ago, Sebra had journeyed up the Sheepscot River to see for himself, and had returned full of excitement. He had met a few settlers, and they had spoken with pride of their independence. "Liberty Men," they called themselves, and they were willing and able to defend their homesteads from the demands of those claiming unjust title.[9] Other settlements had been pressured into submission, but *they* had driven surveyors away three times, destroying their tools and their papers. Patricktown, they said, belonged to the people.

Lydia had listened doubtfully, questioning the security of such a move, but Sebra had already decided. In the fall, he had returned to Patricktown and cleared several acres, leaving the felled trees to burn the following spring. With the children to look after, Lydia had kept her doubts to herself, instead preparing them for the new life ahead. They would all have to work hard and learn a lot, but she was not afraid of work, and she knew Sebra longed for more independence. Nor would they be alone for long; she knew many families who were talking of moving inland.

Drawn out of her thoughts by the boys' shouts, she looks ahead into the forest. They have walked into the evening, and the lowering shadows blur her sight. Still, the trees ahead seem thinner . . .

Stepping into the clearing, Lydia stops, startled by this first glimpse of her new home. Surrounded by the green walls of the forest, the clearing is stark black, thickly coated in ash. Ash, Sebra has told her, will be good for the crops, but it is hard to imagine a farm in such a desolate place. Only blackened stumps remain, defiantly circling the small log cabin that Sebra has built as a temporary shelter.[10]

Lydia's stomach turns, and she brushes her dress nervously, feeling the small bump growing underneath. How can she make a home for five children here, much less welcome a new baby? Lifting her head, she looks around, searching for her straggling brood. Her eldest daughter stands on the far side of the clearing, the cautious but curious sheep pressing against her. The small girls are still asleep in the cart, oblivious to their arrival.

Only the boys are astray. A sudden movement draws her gaze to the middle of the clearing where the fallen trees huddle most tightly. There is a scramble, a muffled shout, and the boys emerge, covered in soot. As proud as they are dirty, they stand atop a fallen giant, surveying their claim without reservation, and she cannot help but laugh. Perhaps there is a home here, she thinks, albeit a messier one. With a determined smile, she steps into the clearing, lifting her skirt to clear the soot.

Drawn to the wilderness by the hope of a better future, they have left behind the conveniences and comforts of colonial life. Now they arrive with a homesteader's tools: an ax, scythe, and grindstone, sturdy pots, and a spinning wheel.[11] Although America is already urbanizing, they have not yet forgotten the capabilities of their hands or the potential of the land.

The land is as yet a forest, a resource in its own right, and it knows nothing of being a farm, but it has been chosen, and it will learn. Soon they will set to work, for seeds must be planted and crops harvested before the onslaught of winter. The trees, valuable in their own right, will be the basis of their new life, for this is a wooden world. Not only furniture but dishes and even tools—shovels[12] and pitchforks—will have to be carved by hand.

Their farm and home grow together, for in this world one is not possible without the other. Fortunately, the summer days are long, but even so, there are never enough hours between sunrise and sunset. Their first home, built entirely by hand, is small and simple, the felled logs squared only at the corners, then laid crossbeam and chinked together with clay. Only the floor is split and hewn from the pliant—and abundant—basswood that yields so easily to the ax. The single room is no more than sixteen by twenty feet, yet serves all their needs. Here they cook, eat, and sleep, their world revolving around the large fireplace that transforms all their labors into sustenance. Away from the fire, the house is dimly lit, its few small windows, covered with oiled paper, reluctantly trading heat for light.[13]

As quickly as trees are cut and laid for the cabin, so crops are planted among the stumps. Sebra and Lydia have chosen carefully, bringing with them the well-adapted seeds of native plants: corn, pumpkin, beans, and potatoes. A handful of apple seeds are planted nearby to be set around the cabin once they have proven strong enough for the Maine winters. Pigs are left to forage in the forest, obligingly fattening themselves on acorns and roots.

But crops and stock take time to grow and, for that first summer, the forest and river are the mainstays of the table. Fish and game of all sorts, from deer and bear to raccoons and pigeons, are the primary sources of protein, and wild plants, especially blueberries, provide valuable sources of vitamins.[14] Even their livestock rely on the native abundance. Someday there will be enough open land to plant English hay,[15] but for now Sebra cuts the wild marsh hay along the river to supplement the browse[16] that the animals forage for themselves.

Looking always toward the future, Sebra opens land for the next year early in the summer. The felled trees must have time to dry thoroughly before they are burned, so that their rich ashes can feed next year's crop. To speed the endless work of clearing, long lines of trees are scored on one side so that with the felling of one key tree, each topples the next in succession,[17] in a giant's game of dominoes.

Corn grows well in the freshly cleared land, and all varieties of beans: Windsor, kidney, Canada, scarlet.[18] Newly burned land yields an abundance of potatoes, up to a hundred bushels per acre, with a variety for every taste: orange, purple, flour, cranberry, bunker, and winter white.[19] Corn and beans, pumpkins and potatoes, these the land knows, and if the hands that plant them are different, the plants themselves know only the delight of the sun and rain and grow with abundance, nourishing these new farmers with native foods.

By the time the crops have matured, their cabin is also finished, and the family turns to putting up the harvest in preparation for the winter. Without a cellar to cool the newly harvested crops, they must be dried to keep from spoiling. Fortunately, the loft is hot and dry, and long strings of corn soon sway above sacks of dried beans. Even pumpkins are cut and hung to dry, their golden flesh the only sweetener readily available. Potatoes, requiring moister, cooler conditions, are buried in a small hole outside.[20] As the temperature drops, the pig, grown "about as large as a good big porcupine,"[21] is slaughtered and carefully preserved. The rich meat is salted and smoked, yielding hams, bacon, and barrels of salt pork to enliven winter's meager fare.

Then there is winter, with no way around it but straight on through. It is cold, often bitterly so, and darkness descends early, confining them to their cabin. Light and heat as well as food are carefully doled out, for winter permits no excesses. Only the fire eats endlessly, noisily, and yet the house is never warm, the walls too thin to hold the heat.

During the short winter days, Sebra heads into the forest, searching the snow-covered boughs for broken or dead branches, food for this year's fire. With winter's chill frozen into his bones, Sebra does not forget next year; when time permits, he chops living trees to dry for the following season.

Tending the hearth, Lydia coaxes what magic she can from their hard-earned harvest. Small chunks of salt pork are stirred into earthenware pots of beans and slow-cooked, while potatoes, baked in the ashes, help stave off the impatience of hunger.[22] The dried corn is ground by hand into Indian meal, then mixed with water and boiled in a cloth bag for several hours. Smooth and dense, the resulting Indian pudding can be eaten hot or cold,[23] and if it does not enliven the taste buds, at least it quells hunger's pangs. Such is winter's fare: food coaxed from forest soils and cooked in chimneys, more water than spice, "pease porridge hot, pease porridge cold, pease porridge in the pot . . ."

Still, they have one great advantage. Although a carpenter by trade, Sebra has always been fascinated with medicine, which he studied with his uncle, Dr. Elijah Crooker, and then their Newcastle neighbor, Dr. Marius How. Medical knowledge is a rare commodity in those times and locations,[24] and the other twenty-two families in Patricktown[25] readily accept "Dr. Crooker" as a physician. He barters his services for food, supplementing their own dwindling stocks as winter drags on.[26]

Lydia has her own reasons to be thankful for Sebra's skills. On January 27, 1809, she feels the unmistakable pangs of labor and stops Sebra on his way out the door. "Stay home today," she says, and though her voice is quiet, her eyes shine and her hand trembles on his shoulder. By evening, she can no longer stand, so, attended by her husband, she lies on their bed, their small world constricting even further.

Aware of the other children's nervous rustling, she stifles her cries, biting down on her lips. Then the darkness presses on the walls of the cabin, engulfing her, and she knows only her own battle. Sometime in the indistinguishable night, she sees her daughter's face for the first time. Illuminated by candle, Julia is a small light in the engulfing blackness of midwinter, the child of their new land.

Despite the promise of a new year and a new baby, winter is inflexible, relishing her reign. The months creep by slowly, demanding their due in cold and darkness. Only with the shifting of the light does winter grudgingly secede, drawing back an inch at a time.

But finally spring is undeniable, and life buzzes with activity. There is more land to clear and new crops to plant. Far from a town, the family's well-being depends directly on their harvest, and the best way to ward off hunger is to tend a diverse mix of crops and stock.[27] Rye replaces some of the corn, and clover and timothy are planted for additional livestock. A cow provides a whole larder of dairy products, from fresh milk and butter to aged hard cheeses. Sheep are essential for their wool, which, along with flax, is spun and woven into cloth for the growing children. With a year's experience, the full value of the forest is revealed. In the spring there is the sweet gift of maple syrup, and beechnuts and butternuts in the fall.

With the addition of rye, the cornmeal finally holds together to make a passable dough. Leavened with local wild yeasts, the large rounded loaves of "rye 'n Injun"[28] bread are baked directly on the hearth.[29] The Indian pudding, now enriched by the addition of milk, eggs, and maple syrup, is no longer merely a survival food, and can be baked alongside the beans instead of boiled.

A Nice Indian Pudding, No. 2[30]

3 pints scalded milk to 1 pint meal, salted. Cool, add 2 eggs, 4 ounces
butter, sugar or molasses (Author's note: or maple syrup!), and spice. It
will require two and a half hours' baking.

If survival seems a little easier, there are other challenges to be faced. Their land, in fact, is not unclaimed territory, but part of the Plymouth Patent, a vast tract of land bestowed by King George to the Plymouth Company in 1620. Stretching for fifteen miles along either side of the Kennebec River, the Plymouth Patent had remained largely undeveloped, passing without much notice to the Kennebec Company in 1753.[31]

After the war, despite settlers' hopes, the new American courts did not confiscate the deeds of the largely Loyalist landowners. Now the Kennebec Proprietors were refocusing on their frontier lands, determined to extract a profit from the many small homesteaders who claimed "possession rights" in defiance of legal claims. It was a heated battle, based on ideas of independence and rights newly tested in the Revolutionary War.

To establish their boundaries, the Proprietors sent in surveyors and formed commissions to pressure settlers into paying.[32] Settlers, bound together in moral certitude, were equally determined to resist what they felt were unjust claims. Calling themselves Liberty Men, they used scare tactics to drive out surveyors and deputies. Elaborately disguised, settlers quickly banded together when word of invading officials was spread, and they just as quickly melted back into their forests and farms afterward.

In this way, the residents of Patricktown prevented Ephraim Ballard from completing his survey in 1795, and again in 1802. Frustrated, Ballard abandoned his survey, and the southeast corner of "Ballard's Line" (delineating the southeast border of the Plymouth Patent) was drawn by directional reference, without a formal survey.[33] Determined, the Kennebec Proprietors hired a new surveyor. In 1810 James Marr was commissioned to finish the survey of the southeast corner. As before, he was obstructed by armed and disguised settlers,[34] who may or may not have included members of the Crooker family.

It is land worth fighting for, as Sebra has chosen well, settling on one of the better pieces of land in Patricktown. At the narrow, hilly end—or rather, the beginning—of the Sheepscot watershed, the little settlement of Patricktown has more ledge and swamp than arable farmland.[35] But as Sebra slowly clears the trees, revealing the contours of their land, they realize that they have, indeed, found a farm. Sloping gently up from the river bottom, the land invites with its soft curves, and the soil, if not deep, can still support hayfields and gardens.

Slowly and laboriously, the soil is opened for the plow, transforming the landscape from a pioneer's patchwork to a farmer's rolling fields. Rocks, of which the land was generously endowed, are piled onto stoneboats[36] and—propelled by the herculean insistence of oxen—dragged to the borders of the field. Here Sebra begins the slow definition of his fields, carefully building the stone walls that will be an enduring part of his legacy, a testament to his patience and skill.

With the stones cleared, there are numerous, and massive, stumps to remove, through a combination of wrangling and burning. Nor does the soil yield herself easily, especially to the pioneer's plow. Hand hewn from a tough tree butt, the colonial bull plow is made entirely from wood, acquiring an iron point only when finances allow. Tackling fresh sod, it works best with two pairs of oxen and three men. "One man drove the oxen; one man stood on the beam, when he could, to hold it down; and the other held the handles. Even then the plow did more rooting than it did plowing. The condition of the newly broken field may well be imagined."[37]

Lydia, likewise, has a formidable task. Six children need not only food but also clothes and, soon, education. Clothes she can and does make herself, transforming the raw wool and flax into coarse but durable linsey-woolsey.[38] It is a lengthy process and, with six active and rapidly growing children, the wheel and loom are always busy. Then there is education. Watching baby Julia toddle around the yard, Lydia wonders what her future will be.

As yet there is no school in Patricktown, although several families have talked of hiring a teacher to live in. The boys know more about working the land than reading, and Lydia's pack of sturdy pioneer girls can already help with the harvest but know little of society.

Lydia smiles, thinking of their eagerness to learn. They are always at her elbow, and she has shown them how to make candles and soap from the pig's fat. This is a different world, one her parents surely never imagined for her; why, here, even a pig's whiskers have a use.[39] At least her children would have land, if they wanted it, and the skills necessary to make a living off it.[40]

The farm prospers, the family grows, and the insecurity of settlement seems far behind them. Yet farm life is always uncertain, for it relies on the unpredictable benevolence of nature. In the spring of 1816, Sebra and Lydia wait for the weather to turn, knowing that corn and pumpkins need a long growing season. May remains stubbornly cool, then June, and finally there can be no more delay; the seeds must go in.

Summer arrives, at least in name, but on July 5, the temperature drops so low that ice forms on the river. Surveying their blackened garden, they know there will be neither corn nor pumpkins that year. Then another frost on August 5 kills the remaining tender crops. They are dismayed but do not despair. As a doctor, Sebra will always have work; things will be tight but not hopeless.

Other families are not so lucky; without alternatives, they cannot face winter without a full larder. Thousands abandon their homesteads and migrate west, beaten by the year "eighteen hundred and froze to death."

Four years away from becoming a state, Maine has already earned a reputation as a risky place to farm.[41]

For those who stay, 1816 brings a different type of hurdle. Unbeknownst to many, the Plymouth Company dissolves, and their unsold lands are purchased by Reuel Williams and Horatio Bridge, former lawyers for the Kennebec Proprietors.[42] Their intimate knowledge of the case, combined with their legal acumen, finally succeeds where others had failed, and surveys are pressed into the last resisting towns. In 1818, Charles Hayden and Joseph Norris successfully complete a survey of Patricktown, giving the new Kennebec Proprietors what they need to press ejectment suits.[43]

Despite Maine's separation from Massachusetts in 1820, the new state legislature looks no more favorably on settlers' claims. Instead, they pass "a stern new law" which makes it easier to try suspected squatters; if convicted, they are "ejected from their homesteads with no right of appeal."[44]

Armed with such tools, Reuel Williams forces the remaining towns to concede to his claims. Beginning in 1821, Reuel focuses his attention on Patricktown, newly organized as a plantation of three hundred people.[45] Of the fifty-two resident households, forty-five are farms[46]—and forty-three are on land claimed by Reuel!

It is a bitter pill for Sebra to swallow, and he watches with frustration as more and more homesteaders are forced to pay. In April 1824, in a last attempt to secure his claim, he makes out a deed to his son, William Crooker, now a man of twenty-three, selling him two hundred acres, including the land on which he lives, for $700.[47] Whether or not money actually changes hands is known only to the father and son.

However, his attempted validation is ignored, and Sebra's sons ultimately must pay the price their father refused. On Christmas Day, 1824, William Crooker, son of Sebra, pays Reuel $288 for the same portion of land that his father had deeded to him eight months earlier, now recorded as "part of lot 18, according to the survey by Hayden & Norris." Sebra Jr., now twenty-four, shares a similar fate. On the same day, he pays Reuel $144 for the ninety-six acres on which he lives.[48]

Systematically Reuel presses his case against the people of Patrick-town, and slowly they pay his price.[49] They have put their dreams and their sweat into the land, and it is finally legally theirs, in the eyes of *all* men. If it is not the freedom they hoped for as Liberty Men, they at least have claim to the foundation of independence: a piece of earth, to grow their families on.

NOTES

1. The exact year of Sebra and Lydia's move to Patricktown cannot be veri-fied, but available historical records suggest a date around this time. Although family oral history recounts their arrival in Patricktown in 1801, the 1800 US Census lists Sebra as a resident of Newcastle, Maine. As late as 1808, multiple deed transfers list Sebra Crooker as a "shipwright of Newcastle." In that year, he sold his last piece of land in Newcastle and disappeared from the historical record! Sebra Crooker is not listed in the 1810 US census, neither in Newcastle, Patricktown, Balltown, or any of the surrounding settlements. In 1820, Sebra resurfaces as a resident of Patricktown. Because of their fear of losing land, set-tlers in that particular corner of Patricktown actively resisted surveys and quite possibly enumeration. Thus it is highly possible that Sebra was not counted in the 1810 census of Patricktown.

2. Clarence Albert Day, *History of Maine Agriculture, 1604–1860* (Orono, ME: University Press, 1954), p. 70. "Maine experienced her most rapid growth between 1784–1810, when more than two thousand new settlers came into the District every year."

3. H. Russell, *A Long, Deep Furrow: Three Centuries of Farming in New Eng-land* (Hanover, NH: University Press of New England, 1982), p. 114.

4. W. H. Bunting, *A Day's Work: A Sampler of Historic Maine Photographs 1860–1920, Part I* (Gardiner, ME: Tilbury House, 1997), pp. 26, 30; Tim Harri-gan, Richard Roosenberg, Dulcy Perkins, and John Sarge, *Estimating Ox-Drawn Implement Draft* (Kalamazoo, MI: Tillers International, 2011). Recent research estimates the speed of an ox team on a gravel road as slightly over two miles per hour. This agrees with historic accounts of how far a loaded team had traveled in a day (e.g., forty-four miles in a long, twenty-six-hour haul to and from a seaport).

5. Both Sebra and Lydia were born in Pembroke, Massachusetts, in the county of Plymouth. In 1794, Sebra, a "ship carpenter from Marshfield" (just east of Pembroke), bought his first piece of land in Newcastle. In 1799 he

married Lydia Curtis. Information gathered from deeds housed at the Lincoln County Registry of Deeds and state records of Massachusetts accessed via Ancestry.com.

6. Alan Taylor, *Liberty Men and Great Proprietors* (Chapel Hill: University of North Carolina Press, 1990), pp. 62–65. "Population growth and careless exploitation had wrought worsening scarcities of land, hay, fish . . . lumber, timber and firewood in southern New England's old towns . . . Most emigrated from small towns on or near the coast (such as Plymouth) . . . most came from poor families . . . the quickest and cheapest route to the frontier was by sea to the coast of Maine . . . a day's sail brought a family from Boston to mid-Maine . . . in 1801 passage . . . cost two dollars, the equivalent of four days' wages for a laborer."

7. Between 1794 and 1808, deeds housed at the Lincoln County Registry of Deeds record Sebra's purchase and sale of numerous pieces of land in Newcastle, Edgecombe, Camden, and Bristol.

8. Taylor, *Liberty Men and Great Proprietors*, p. 15.

9. Ibid., p. 95. The Liberty Men's credo went as follows: "God gave the earth to the children. We own no other proprietor. Wild land ought to be as free as common air. These lands once belonged to King George. He lost them by the American Revolution and they became the property of the people who defended and won them. The General Court did wrong and what they had no right to do when they granted them in such large quantities to certain companies and individuals and the bad acts of government are not binding on the subject."

10. Ibid., pp. 64–65.

11. Day, *History of Maine Agriculture*, p. 71.

12. Russell, *A Long, Deep Furrow*, p. 103. "Their shovels were likely to be fashioned from a thick plank, suitably hollowed at one end . . . It was a disadvantage in a frontier settlement to own a shovel shod with iron, because of the temptation for neighbors to borrow it!"

13. Richard W. Judd, Edwin A. Churchill, and Joel W. Eastman (eds.), *Maine: The Pine Tree State from Prehistory to the Present* (Orono: University of Maine Press, 1995), p. 246.

14. Day, *History of Maine Agriculture*, p. 44.

15. Ibid., p. 42; Russell, *A Long, Deep Furrow*, p. 150. English hay consisted of a mixture of timothy, redtop, and red and white clover, introduced by English settlers as preferred hay species.

16. Day, *History of Maine Agriculture*, p. 42. "Browse might be a mixture of bushes and weeds, but more often it was boughs of softwood trees, hemlock, or pine by preference."

17. Ibid., p. 43.

18. Reverend Samuel Deane, *The New-England farmer; or, Georgical dictionary. Containing a compendious account of the ways and methods in which the important art of husbandry, in all its various branches, is, or may be, practiced, to the greatest advantage, in this country* (Boston: Wells and Lilly, 1822), as referenced in Day, *History of Maine Agriculture*, p. 91.

19. Ibid.

20. Keith Stavely and Kathleen Fitzgerald, *America's Founding Food* (Chapel Hill: University of North Carolina Press, 2004), pp. 125, 126.

21. Day, *History of Maine Agriculture*, p. 45.

22. Stavely and Fitzgerald, *America's Founding Food*, p. 57.

23. Ibid., p. 12.

24. Russell, *A Long, Deep Furrow*, p. 112.

25. Ancestry.com. *1810 United States Federal Census* [online database]. Provo, UT, USA: Ancestry.com Operations, Inc., 2009. Images reproduced by FamilySearch.

26. Stavely and Fitzgerald, *America's Founding Food*, p. 125.

27. Ibid., p. 124: ". . . produced and preserved for themselves a great deal of what they needed in the way of food and the other necessities of life through a 'safety first' mixed rather than staple cash crop agriculture."

28. Day, *History of Maine Agriculture*, p. 54.

29. Stavely and Fitzgerald, *America's Founding Food*, p. 25.

30. Amelia Simmons, *American Cookery*, 1st ed. (Hartford, CT: 1796). Reprint, with an introduction by Mary Tolford Wilson (New York: Dover, 1958). As cited in Stavely and Fitzgerald, *America's Founding Food*, p. 15.

31. From: http://jamesdaly.info/historical-background, accessed October 2013. The Plymouth Patent was a grant made to the Plymouth Company (of *Mayflower* fame) in 1620 and revised in 1630. In this revision, the Plymouth Company was granted "all that Tract of Land or part of New England in America aforesaid which lyeth within or betweene and Extendeth it Selfe from the utmost of Cobestcont alias Comasecont Which adjoyneth to the River Kenibeck alias Kenebeckick towards the Westerne Ocean and a place called the falls of Nequamkick in America aforesaid and the Space of fifteen English miles on Each Side of the said River Comonly called Kenebeck River . . ." In 1753 the Kennebec Company (aka, the Kennebec Proprietors) purchased the Patent.

32. Taylor, *Liberty Men and Great Proprietors*, p. 121: "Unless deputy sheriffs could serve writs on settlers and unless proprietary surveyors could run their lines proving that the defendants dwelled within a particular claim, proprietors could not successfully prosecute the ejectment and trespass cases necessary to reestablish their control."

33. From: http://jamesdaly.info/historical-background, accessed October 2013. "Proprietors commissioned Ephraim Ballard to survey the full length of the eastern boundary line. Starting from the north, Ballard was able to survey the line down to the point where it intersected with the western boundary of the Waldo Patent . . . Ballard continued the survey southward at an angle of S31W until he reached a point near to what is now Jones Corner along Rte 17. Here, he was attacked by settlers who believed his surveys would result in their losing their lands. They destroyed his notes and his survey equipment, and he was forced to abandon his efforts, swearing never to return (1793, and again, 1802). The remaining portion of the Gore's western boundary was thenceforward deemed to run due south until it struck the Jefferson line."

34. Taylor, *Liberty Men and Great Proprietors*, p. 278.

35. Allard, French, Cranmer, and Milakovsky, *Then & Now: Patricktown/ Somerville, Volume Two: History* (Somerville, ME: Somerville Historical Society, 2008) p. 3.

36. Day, *History of Maine Agriculture*, p. 52; Russell, *A Long, Deep Furrow*, p. 102; Harrigan et al., *Estimating Ox-Drawn Implement Draft*, p. 4. Stoneboats are flat sledges or drags purposefully built without runners. Since they are close to the ground, it is easy to roll (rather than lift) heavy boulders onto them. Their wide bottom spreads the load, increasing the ease with which you can pull them over a tilled field.

37. Day, *History of Maine Agriculture*, pp. 52 and 135: "Elderly men of later days had painful memories of that old plow of wood. With Alfred Cushman, of Golden Ridge, they might say: 'Well do I remember the first plow I ever held . . . and my vain attempts to keep the thing in the ground; and when I denounced it as worthless, Grandfather said, "It is an excellent plow."'"

38. Day, *History of Maine Agriculture*, p. 56.

39. Stavely and Fitzgerald, *America's Founding Food*, p. 177. (Pig's whiskers were used as brushes.)

40. Ibid., p. 124: "The purpose of just about everything that took place on the New England family farm was to perpetuate . . . a landed freedom and independence that seemed to be growing increasingly elusive."

41. Russell, *A Long, Deep Furrow*, p. 147.

42. Ibid., p. 246.

43. From an original 1818 survey conducted by Charles Hayden and Joseph Norris, housed at the Lincoln County Registry of Deeds. Also from Taylor, *Liberty Men and Great Proprietors*, pp. 226–27.

44. Taylor, *Liberty Men and Great Proprietors*, p. 241.

45. http://www.themrscott.com/City,_Town,_Plantation.html, accessed November 2013. "Plantations are a unique local government in Maine. They originated in the Massachusetts Bay Colony. Since then, they have been discarded by other states as a type of local government. Plantations were first intended to be a temporary kind of government to guide a community in changing from an unincorporated township to an incorporated township. But in Maine, they have continued as a basic governmental unit.

Plantations are similar to towns in that the annual meeting is the governing body of the town. But plantations are different from towns in two major ways: First, they are organized by the vote of the county commissioners in the county in which they are located, while towns are incorporated by vote of the State Legislature; second, they do not have the powers granted to towns under Maine's Home Rule law. Under Home Rule, towns may take any action or change their form of government in any way that is not clearly denied them or provided for under state and/or federal law. Plantations are mostly rural, heavily forested, and sparsely populated communities. There is little demand in them for all the public services provided in larger communities."

46. Ancestry.com. *1820 United States Federal Census* [online database]. Provo, UT: Ancestry.com Operations, Inc., 2009. Images reproduced by FamilySearch.

47. From deed, Sebra Crooker to William Crooker, housed in the Lincoln County Registry of Deeds.

48. From deeds housed in the Lincoln County Registry of Deeds.

49. Ibid. By 1860, all forty-three settlers pay Reuel for a deed to their land, thirty-two of which are subsequently mortgaged to him. In 1829, Sebra finally pays for a deed to his land, but only indirectly to Reuel; he pays his son William for half of the land William bought from Reuel in 1824.

October 2009

Harvest

As the days grow shorter and darker, the leaves increase in brilliance, burning with the stored radiance of the summer sun. I point the trees out to Keiran, his world bursting with colors and shapes noticed for the first time. Our walks have slowed as he stops to collect leaves from the road, as intrigued by the curled brown ones as the brilliant red.

With the cooling days comes the opportunity to butcher our pigs. We had planned to send them to a local butcher, but we had not expected to need reservations; with regret, they inform us that there are no openings until January. Although we had slaughtered goats before, the pigs, at more than two hundred pounds per animal, are on a different scale altogether. Anil, however, did not earn his award for practical farm skills for naught; undaunted, he merely seeks reinforcements.

Prevailing upon the good nature of our friends, we set the date for mid-month and get busy with preparations. I read up on curing and smoking, while my husband orders a meat saw and sharpens his knives. Aware of our responsibility to both friends and pigs, I await the day with a mixture of excitement and uncertainty.

The day before the harvest is busy, and, for my part, at least, slightly nerve-racking. Anil spends the day preparing his stations for the various stages of the butchering. Our rickety old picnic table appears on the lawn, conveniently placed in front of our picture window, its legs reinforced and a sheet of metal nailed to the top. It looks precarious and rather shabby, and I wonder if we know what we are doing.

Anil is still assembling the meat saw when I put Keiran to bed, and, descending into the root cellar, I fight the insidious despair of fatigue. However, as I peel and slice potatoes, a sense of celebration returns. There is something fitting in this work, preparing food into the night for this gathering of life around death.

The next morning is cool and clear, and our friends John and David arrive invigorated, accepting coffee and doughnuts more for indulgence than fortification. Keiran has his own schedule for the day, and as the men head out, I take him upstairs for his nap. He has been slightly fever-ish, and he rolls in his crib, seeking the comfort of my hand. When he finally settles, I creep next door and am drawn with dread and curiosity to pull back the heavy quilted curtains that face the back fields.

I see only one pig, but I hear the men's voices in the shed and then, muted, the short pop of the stun gun. The stun gun had been Anil's concession to my concerns about humane slaughter, and we had spent a large amount of our limited funds to purchase a quality tool. By pen-etrating the brain, the stun gun causes instant brain death while the heart is still beating. This allows the necessary bleeding to occur when the pig's throat is cut, ensuring the quality of the meat, without any awareness on the animal's part. In this case, the pig had surrendered without a single one of its notorious squeals, and we are all relieved and grateful.

A few seconds later, the men emerge, pulling hard against the dead weight of the downed pig. The field is wet, and the pig's back is soon slick with mud. Although I know the pig is brain-dead, it is still disturbing to see its hind legs kicking, the men struggling to keep hold. With obvious effort, they pull it up a small hill and out of the pen, then slide it quickly down the smooth grass to the "bleeding" station. Anil bends over the neck, knife in hand, but I am saved from my voyeuristic initiation by the sound of Keiran crying. Dropping the curtain, I return to his room, where he sits forlornly, waiting for me to soothe him.

By the time I return downstairs the pig is front and center stage. Somehow the men have hoisted it onto the picnic table, which, amazingly, has not collapsed. Up for the weekend, my brother Alex and sister-in-law Kathy, rising late from their beds, are ambivalent about the sight that greets them on their entry into the living room. However, despite their pointed nonchalance, it is hard to ignore the outdoor activities, and Kathy remarks with surprise, "They seem to be having fun!"

When Keiran wakes, we all head outside, inexorably drawn to the show. The pig rests on its side while the men wash the mud away, and I am surprised at how normal it all seems. The sun is starting to touch the frosty air with warmth, and the men are in high spirits, guessing the pig's weight. Only as I round the table and glimpse the gaping neck wound do I pause, facing the full reality of life drained away.

Keiran, heedless of the pig's carcass, circles around the table, proud to be at the center of activities. Forbidden from touching the knives, he looks with interest at the blood pooling on the dirt, until I decide to move him to safer ground. Pointing out other delights, I tempt him higher up the lawn where we can watch without total sensory immersion.

As the men hold the legs apart, Anil makes a delicate cut along the belly, and the skin slides open, revealing layers of fat and muscle. Another stroke and he reaches in, separating organs from skin. He is graceful, moving with deliberate precision, and I am surprised to find beauty in the moment. His hands are gentle as he moves along the body, transforming the raw life of the pig into the sustenance of our bodies. Here, closer than I have ever been to the taking of life, I understand the butcher as artist, shaping life from death.

Burdened by no such philosophical contemplations, Keiran interrupts with the urgent demands of a hungry belly, and I carry him inside in search of a less bloody snack. While he pursues animal crackers around the tray of his high chair, I watch through the window, surprised to see Kathy heading up to the house bearing a large bowl.

Once utterly urban, Kathy has embraced the direct experience of farm life without restraint, her enthusiasm undimmed by the awkward and messy. Now, entering the kitchen, she shows me the contents of the bowl with pride—fresh tenderloin, set aside for dinner.

Although we had planned on serving the tenderloin that night, I realize, peering into the bowl, that I am entering new territory, my expectations bumping into reality. This is not meat from the grocery store, packaged and chilled; this is fresh meat, radiating body heat, its edges raw and quivering. In the confines of the kitchen, the smell of blood is strong, more than I can bear in my pregnant state, and I retreat a step from the proffered bowl.

"What shall we do with it?" Kathy asks, and I wonder along with her, the warm lump of meat an invited but alien guest. My cookbooks had assured me this was the choicest cut, best served fresh, and we had planned a meal around it. But how to preserve its quality until dinner time? Reluctant to refrigerate it, we carry it down to the cellar, its stone walls cool and damp.

By lunchtime, the men have finished the first pig, and they hang the two halves of the carcass in the workshop. Conscious of their blood-stained clothes, I bring chairs and sandwiches to the lawn, and they rest in the sun, analyzing the morning's work with satisfaction. A doctor, a teacher, and an animal scientist, they make an unlikely trio for such an event, but each somehow fits in the relationship. Bound now by common experience, they laugh and kid each other, the grace of friendship sanctifying their work.

After lunch the men head back to the pigpen, checking their watches. Now an experienced team, they plan a speedier exit for the second pig. Meanwhile, my friends Carol and Debbi arrive, and we turn to our work, preparing a meal worthy of the occasion.

While I was planning the event, I had surveyed our neglected garden with dismay, fearing there was not much to draw from. As we fill the plates, however, it suddenly seems a banquet: slices of pork bathed in a tomato cream sauce, wild mushrooms foraged by my brother, potatoes dug the day before, green beans from a friend's garden. Awaiting our observant eye and picking hand, the earth has yielded abundantly. As we pass dishes around the table, we are one long exclamation of delight, our taste buds saturated with freshness.

The next day is more prosaic and more isolating; with the carcasses hanging in the workshop, Anil needs to cut up the meat—and that means Keiran and I are on our own. Anil works all afternoon, bringing up cartload after cartload of meat, strange packages labeled RUMP and SHOULDER.

As I stand in front of our huge, empty freezer, I am flustered, unfamiliar with meat named by body part. Where are my chops and country-style ribs? I don't have recipes for shoulder and butt; whatever will we use them for? Anil is calm in the face of my confusion, helping me sort the meat: This can be used for stew, that for ground, that for chops.

He works steadily, finishing one half, then one hog, steadily filling the freezer. At dinnertime, he is still working, so I throw a frozen pizza in the oven, unable to do more with Keiran in tow. As we carry our offering of love and sustenance down to Anil, I have to laugh at the irony, this juxtaposition of where we are and where we want to be. Still, it is a step, and, with Keiran holding my hand, I am reminded that it is the small steps that will get us to our goal.

OCTOBER 2009

LOVE ETERNAL

MID-OCTOBER and the hard frosts have arrived. Defenseless, the gardens collapse, their blackened stems shrunken against the dirt. Without the urgency of harvest calling me forth, there is a strange quiet, as if the energy of life has somehow receded.

Standing in the fallen garden, I laugh, remembering Shirley's wry comment about their wedding date. She and Don had married in October because it was "the only month we had time to get married." As a farmer, I could appreciate the truth of that statement, but I was equally aware of the steadfast love that had sustained their marriage for fifty-eight years.

A few months earlier, I had caught Don picking his precarious way among the tumbled stone wall, in pursuit of the beautiful but thorny wild roses that Shirley particularly loved. Although Shirley and Don both laugh at the notion that he is a romantic, his love—and her delight—are visible in every gesture and glance. After so many years of marriage, there is still a playful quality to their relationship that inspires those of us just starting out.

With Kathy and Alex as collaborators, we plan an anniversary dinner to celebrate their long-standing love. In preparation, I roast a chicken, mash potatoes, boil squash, bake biscuits—but I know the food will be merely background to the feast of stories and laughter. Nor am I disappointed; bending over the stove to check the biscuits, I hear Kathy laughing as she shows the Hewetts in, Shirley's voice rising in animation.

As they enter the kitchen, life and joy sweeps in with them, and they retell their story, including us in their delight. When she awoke on her anniversary morning, Shirley had turned to Don, sighing wistfully, "I wish I felt like I did the day we were married." Regarding his bride of fifty-eight years with affection, he replied, "I don't know what I'd do with you if you did!"

Standing in the doorway, the warm biscuits in my hands, I watch Don seat Shirley at the table, gently helping her into a chair. It is always special to have them in our house, this house that is more theirs than ours. As I follow them into the dining room, I have the feeling that I am the guest, a child playacting as host. I have seen this same blue-and-white wallpaper in old photos, other faces gathered around the table, and I see them now, as Don pulls up to the table. He has eaten many meals here, shared many celebrations, and I welcome the warm connection of family.

Over dinner we ask questions, catching up with each other's news, but more often than not our stories, so vivid in their retelling, lead to the past. They laugh, telling us about the letter they had received addressed to "The Tractors," delivered without hesitation by the post office. As much as they are a part of the farm, so the farm has become a part of them, in public and private identity.

Before we bought the farm, other families had passed through, but none of them had stayed long. The farm had cast its spell over one young girl, however, its enchantment forever woven into her dreams, her soul.

Since she was a baby, Kate Hassett had been fascinated by Don, watching as he drove the tractor back and forth across the fields. As she learned to talk, she watched him earnestly, working her tongue around the syllables of his name. Seeing him entering the room, she pointed, proud of her newfound skill. "Tractor," she proclaimed.

The name had stuck, and when Kate moved away, a letter soon arrived in the mailbox, to be followed by many others, addressed to the Tractors of Hewett Road. Through Don, Kate had discovered the magic of the farm, and the connection remained, with the power to shape lives; now in adulthood, she too longed to farm.

I sigh in satisfaction, another mystery of the farm solved. I had stumbled on the story myself during a frenzy of cleaning in the early months of ownership. Brushing cobwebs from the garage wall, I had almost erased the childish scrawl of *Tractor* enclosed in a heart, the delicate chalk somehow surviving the wear of time. Then I had noticed *Kate* and *Elizabeth* on the opposite wall, their names in the same red chalk, and I had stayed my hand as if warded off by some childish magic.

Deep in stories, we remember dessert only because of its promise. Shirley has brought over an apple pie, and we come gladly back to the present, eager for the anticipated delight. In a region famous for its apple pies, Shirley's outshines them all. A perfect balance of sweet and tart, the apples hold their shape but yield without resistance to the eager bite. And the crust—the crust is sublime, the perfect cradle for the apples, substantial enough to feel without being tough.

Shirley laughs at our praise, remembering her difficulties when she was first married. Other women had told her they didn't make pies because they couldn't make a good crust. But Don had said his favorite apple was one in a crust, and so she kept trying, rolling out the delicate dough, laying it over the apples, each time a little better. Now the crust threatened to outshine the apples, and she strived simply to maintain her standard.

SHIRLEY HEWETT'S APPLE PIE RECIPE,
FOR A TWO-CRUST PIE:

Preheat oven to 350 degrees. Stir a pinch of salt into 2 cups flour, then add 1 ½ cups shortening, working in with your hands until crumbly. Set your faucet at a dribble, then put the bowl under and mix the water in until the dough barely holds together, being careful not to add too much. Divide into two balls, with the bottom crust slightly larger than the top crust. Roll the bottom crust out and lay in a pie pan.

Take 4 or 5 good-size apples, preferably Cortlands or Northern Spies (a great keeper), although any apple will do. Quarter them, core them, and cut each quarter into 4 slices. Taste the apples to check their sweetness, adding more or less than ⅓ cup sugar. Mix in cinnamon and nutmeg to taste. Fill the crust with the apples, then lay the top crust on, pricking with a fork. Bake for at least 45 minutes, or until the crust is golden brown and the juices are showing up a little. Although nowadays people like ice cream, this pie is also fine served by itself.

So thoroughly had Shirley learned her way around the kitchen that it soon became solely her domain. Although Don would attempt to help out if she was sick, "It would take him so long to peel a potato, I'd feel sorry for him." We all laugh, and Don half rises. "I think I'd better be leaving before she starts to tell more stories about me," he protests in mock dread, but his eyes are twinkling.

Still, the evening has sped by while we were talking, and soon he rises to leave in earnest. Leaning on the table, he pauses, looking at us with affection and pride. "You can be like us someday," he says, turning his gentle gaze on each of us, snuggled comfortably next to our mates. "You both have a good start." From him, it is a compliment, an affirmation of our relationships, but more than that, it is a blessing, his own joy shining forth as he stands beside Shirley.

We delay the inevitable moment of parting, slipping in one last story, one last laugh as we walk them out. Slowly we release them to their car, their own private world, feeling our bonds of love stretch as they drive down the road, lights receding. Watching them, we stay close together, arms around shoulders and waists.

We are bound to each other by spiderwebs of connection, graceful loops hung heavy with dew, reaching into the past. This is their home and our home and our children's home, their love and our love and our children's love. As we head back inside, the house welcomes us, the wooden floors, polished by the footsteps of generations, warm against our feet.

1830

JULIA AND EPHRAIM KENNEDY

THE ROAD, although narrow, is well established now, allowing the rapid passage of a single young man, Ephraim Kennedy, twenty-five years old. Urging his horse on, he passes the neighboring farms with a wave, eager to reach his new wife.

In a quarter-mile he slows, looking with pride at the small house and barn they have only recently finished. Married last year, they finally have their own home, and just in time, as evident by Julia's swollen belly when she waves from the doorway.

He jumps down onto the road, dusty from the summer heat, and holds up a thin envelope. "A letter," he shouts, "from Samuel."

Although it is daytime, the house, with its small windows, is dimly lit, so they stand in the yard to read the letter. Sent on July 8, 1830, from Newburyport, Massachusetts, it has been carried on horseback along post roads to reach the local office in Jefferson.[1]

Dear brother,[2]
I had the pleasure today to receive your letter and now retire to write to
you. I was at a greate stand when I saw inscribed at the top, Jefferson,

but was very glad to hear from you and that your prospects are promising. But, I do not very well like the place where you have bought your land, for you must sertinly be deprived of many privileges that might be enjoyed elsewhere, for that is a dark corner of the globe and little society to enjoy there . . .

Ephraim laughs, looking around the sunlit clearing, the boards of their house still fresh and shining, their garden in the green fullness of maturity. Although there are still more trees than houses, he prefers it that way. Even on a gray day, the fields and forest never seem as dreary as the streets of town.

And if there are only sixty-eight families[3] in Patricktown, he knows them better than he ever knew his neighbors in Boothbay. They help each other out here, and he has quickly learned who to call on when he needs extra hands.[4] Just up the hill, their barn stands tall and straight, its strong, clean lines a testament to the power of cooperation and the art of human craftsmanship. If there is one thing they are not lacking, it is community.

The strong ties of the Crooker family were already legendary in Patricktown; so many of Sebra's children had settled nearby, the townspeople called their road Crooker Town. Lydia and Mary, they joked, had married neighboring farmers[5] so that they could stay close to home, and William had built an impressive house next door to his parents. Although Mercy had followed her husband to Prentis, and Sebra Jr. had moved to Canada, Ephraim knew that Julia loved her home. When she accepted his offer of marriage, he had willingly looked for land in Patricktown. He himself had been adopted as a child by Sebra's brother Francis, and he felt warmly included in the Crooker family.

Julia nudges him, giggling, and he turns back to his brother's words.

I wish you to write to me often that I may know you get along, and when the boy is born to suppose you must call his name Samuel.

With a tolerant grin, he hugs Julia, supposing he might humor his brother. He is lucky, he thinks, to have such a wife—and such a farm.

Growing up in coastal Boothbay, some forty miles away, he had been more familiar with the sound and smell of the ocean than the ring of an ax and creak of the plow, but he liked the substantial work of building his own home. What he didn't know, Julia was sure to, and his in-laws were eager to help them get a good start. Their prospects seemed good to him, regardless of his brother's dire predictions.

Loosening his saddlebags, he hands Julia the rest of the packages he has brought: the salt, molasses, coffee,[6] and, recently, flour[7] that supplement the provisions they grow. As yet, there is little to be bought locally; stores are far away, reached only by arduous travel over bad roads. For some years it will be up to them to provide their own food, clothing, and shelter; luckily, their neighbors, by circumstance and inclination, are as thrifty and enterprising as they, and always have something to barter in times of need.

Julia takes the letter inside, placing it carefully with their small pile of letters, their link to a rapidly changing outside world. Growing up a pioneer child, she does not miss the conveniences she has never known, but as a wife and expectant mother, she is increasingly aware of the world beyond. Last year her friend Henrietta French had written to her from Canterbury, Massachusetts, on the eve of her wedding to Ephraim.

I hope that I shall hear the good news, that you are also so well and happy. I want to see you very much, but I do not expect to very soon. I have not forgotten the pleasant hours we have spent together. . . . Inform me if you have heard from Mr. E. Kennedy and how he does.

Julia smiles, remembering how they had whispered together over Ephraim's attentions. She will have to write Henrietta soon and tell her that Ephraim had bought a piece of land,[8] a good piece of land with a spring on it, and that she is now a farm wife.

A wife, she thinks, with her own home, and soon, babies! She is not afraid of her new responsibilities, as she had always helped her mother in the house, and life is, in fact, much easier now.

Remembering the one-room cabin she had grown up in, she looks with pride around her own home. Not only is there a separate dining area off the kitchen, but there is also a parlor, neat as a pin and as yet unused. Why, there is even a real upstairs for sleeping, their bed tucked snugly under the sloping roof. It is colder up there than the loft had been, so Ephraim had built a second fireplace, which warms and illuminates their room.[9] The house is better lit now, too, with lamps replacing candles. Whale oil was expensive and smelled unpleasantly fishy, but the new lamps burn as brightly as ten candles, without the smoke of tallow lamps.[10]

She has even heard of iron stoves to cook on, which supposedly heat better than the fireplace and bake better than the brick oven Ephraim had built in the chimney.[11] Her daughters, she thinks, might not need a fireplace, but for herself, she is delighted to bake in her chimney-side brick oven,[12] especially since they can now get wheat flour, which lightened her mother's rye 'n Injun bread. Now commonly known as brown bread,[13] it is to become a staple of New England cookery, still used a hundred years later by her granddaughter.

BROWN BREAD [WRITTEN BY EDITH HEWETT FOR HER DAUGHTER, EARLY 1900s]

Two and one-half cups of sour milk or buttermilk, ½ cup of molasses, salt, about 4 *teaspoonfuls soda according to the sourness of the milk, 3 cups (corn) meal, and 3 cups (wheat) flour. Steam 3 hours or more.*

The tedious work of preparing flax was also a thing of the past,[14] and the mill at Turner's Corner in Whitefield now carded wool,[15] returning it as clean, fluffy rolls, ready to spin.[16] This spring she had even seen men's ready-made shirts and pants in the store at Cooper's Mills. They were expensive, and she was proud to see Ephraim in the clothes she had made, the light blue homespun woven from their own wool.[17] But as her family grew, there would be less time and more need, and she would be glad of some help to keep them all clothed.[18]

Just a few months later, on September 13, 1830, Julia gave birth to their first child, a boy whom they did indeed name Samuel, in deference to the love—if not the lecture—from Ephraim's brother. A daughter, Judith, followed, and then two boys, a next-generation Sebra and Ephraim. The road was busy with the antics of small children running between the houses of cousins and grandparents, delighted adventurers in a seamless world of family and farm.

Then, in the unsuspecting spring of 1839, the inexorable hand of death interrupted the dance, snatching away its senior member. Word traveled down the road that Julia's father, Sebra Sr., had been scalded to death in a tanner's vat in the neighboring town of China.

The family reeled before the impossibility of it, unsure how to proceed without its navigating force. They were here, they realized, because of him. They had followed him, joined him, assembled around him, stayed with him. Now they were here, but he was—gone? It was, as it ever is, an unanswerable absence, and grief did not sit lightly on any of them.

Time did not stop its coil, though, and the daily life of a farm— and, much more, the needs and love of children—drove them on. With ten years of experience, Ephraim was no longer a novice at farming, and looking around him, he realized that a lot had changed since he had moved to Patricktown. The little town was flourishing, as more people moved in and small-scale manufacturing developed to meet their needs. Dams had been built on the many small tributaries of the Sheepscot and Damariscotta rivers that flowed through Somerville, and sawmills had been erected.[19] Even little Jones Brook, which flowed through their property, had a dam. In 1836, Sebra and John had sold Hiram Hook a piece of land along the creek to build a sawmill.[20] Just over four feet wide, the dam powered the up-and-down saw that operated Clifford's mill.[21]

New settlers were building fine houses from the smoothly hewn boards, and older settlers were gradually expanding their previous dwellings. Mill owners, flush with business, "helped finance other home industries, from grist mills to brickyards to tanneries."[22]

With more people there was more traffic, especially since Augusta, their closest city, had become the state capital in 1832. The town had developed a formal network of roads, with local farmers working off their taxes by plowing and scraping the road with their ox teams.[23] It was now possible to reach markets in Augusta and Wiscasset within a day's drive, and Ephraim began to think about selling his surplus crops in the market.

It was a promising time for agriculture, with societies, magazines, books, and fairs all promoting the growth and development of agriculture in Maine. Recently, a neighbor had shown him a book entitled *The New England Farmer*, written by a Maine farmer. Despite being both a reverend and a Harvard graduate, the author, Samuel Deane, was also a working farmer, and had a lot to say on the subject. Some of it made sense to Ephraim, like rotating livestock on pastures, while some of it just seemed like extra work, like pasturing pigs on clover.[24] In Ephraim's opinion, they did just fine foraging for themselves in the woods.

Searching for answers to declining harvests, Ephraim read on with keen interest. With some disbelief, he perused the author's long list of beneficial "manures," which included not only livestock manure, but also feathers, fish, moss, and soapsuds.[25] Remembering his brother's comments, he had to laugh at Deane's lament that "persons of a liberal or polite education should think it intolerably degrading . . . to attend to practical agriculture for their support." On the contrary, the author asserted, farmers should "toss about their dung with an air of majesty."[26]

Grinning at the thought of Samuel "tossing dung," Ephraim was glad that tools, at least, had been, and still were, improving. At least you could actually toss dung on the new wrought-iron forks, unlike the old wooden forks that clung to their load. Thanks to iron, farming was more productive—and, mercifully, less backbreaking. Iron had made possible the development of hoes and hand scythes. Best of all was the addition of cast-iron tips to plows.[27] With the new plows, neither the oxen nor he tired as quickly, and even breaking sod yielded more than a backache. Best of all, there were many more such machines on the way, if the *Maine Farmer* was to be believed.

Ephraim had first seen a copy of this publication at Sebra's house, for his father-in-law, ever a man of science, was as profoundly interested in agriculture as he was in the human body. First published in 1833, the *Maine Farmer* was the primary source of agricultural information in the state. Filled with everything from the latest science to poetry, fiction, and advertisements, it found a place on the kitchen table of most small farms. Here Ephraim read the reports of the many local agricultural societies that had blossomed in the last ten years, and learned who had won prizes at the various agricultural fairs.[28] Everyone, it seemed, was talking about—if not directly involved in—agriculture. Perhaps, he thought, Samuel would eventually respect his profession.

December 14, 1842. Ten days before Christmas, Francis Baxter Kennedy arrived in the world, cold, naked, and bawling. Holding her squalling infant in her arms, Julia was pleased with his forcefulness. Three years after her father's death, there was finally a new life to celebrate, a filling of emptiness. Too familiar now with loss, she held him close, feeling his heart beating against hers. Perhaps, she thought, he would stay . . .

Although she could not know it, Francis would indeed be the one to stay on the farm. Perhaps it was the timing of his birth, so soon after his grandfather's death, that created binding ties, or perhaps it was the great hope in agriculture that pervaded society at the time. Never again would Maine see farming as favorably as it did in the first twenty years of Francis's life. In 1856, Maine formed a board of agriculture, putting state support into the development of the agricultural industry.[29]

Ephraim had kept his eye out for good land, and by 1850 had doubled his holdings, claiming title to two hundred acres in the 1850 Agricultural Census. With so much unbroken land, he needed the draft power of four oxen to clear and plow enough to feed his seven children. Over the course of a year, they grew—and ate!—sixty bushels of corn, forty bushels of oats, twenty bushels of potatoes, and six bushels of peas and beans. Two cows and a pig provided meat, while his four dairy cows produced not only milk for the family, but four hundred pounds of butter a year for trade at the local stores. And, for the first time, Ephraim entered the cash market, raising eight sheep and selling twenty-two pounds of wool to the woolen market. All that stock required its own maintenance—namely, eighteen tons of hay to cut, cure, and pack by hand.[30]

Like Ephraim, many other Maine farmers began to shift to commercial crops, swayed by the state's increasing integration with the rest of the nation. The rapid development of the railroad, starting in the 1850s, brought increased competition as well as greater access to markets. As the railroad spread into the interior of Maine, inland farmers suddenly had an alternative to the distant seaport.

With easier access to cheap produce from Western farms, Maine farmers lost the incentive to grow everything themselves, focusing instead on supplying the burgeoning Boston market, as well as Maine's own growing cities. As farmers expanded their operations, they were quick to take advantage of advances in agricultural technology. Horse-drawn mowers, rakes, and threshers freed farmers from manual labor, but, bought on credit, further tied them to the cash economy.[31]

Like Maine, the population of Patricktown had also doubled by mid-century. The 107 families[32] now included many tradespeople: three mill men, three carpenters, two coopers, two traders, and a shoemaker. The town boasted not only a clergyman and a physician (William Crooker, taught by his father, Sebra), but also seven schools spread out so that all children had a school within walking distance. For Francis and his six siblings, the small schoolhouse at the end of their road was only a mile away, a short distance for country children.

Patricktown was, in fact, "settled," no longer a frontier outpost but an established village, with all the requisite community services. By 1857 it had two general stores, two blacksmith shops, three cooper's shops, and five sawmills, as well as a shingle mill and a stave mill.[33] To mark its passage to a developed community, it left behind the name of Patricktown in 1858, taking its place among the incorporated towns of Maine under the hopeful name of Somerville.

The future seemed good for small Maine farming communities such as Somerville, even if the assessment of their potential was based on slightly enhanced claims. As the Belfast newspaper, *The Progressive Age*, described Somerville, "The new town has more than an average amount of good farming land, good water privileges, and other means of wealth, as well as a large number of intelligent, respectable, and fore-handed men."[34] For this generation, at least, Somerville, Maine, seemed a promising place to farm.

NOTES

1. From Sterling T. Dow, *Maine Postal History and Postmarks* (Lawrence, MA: Quarterman Publications, 1976). Under the American postal system, "a line of posts was appointed from Falmouth (Portland, Maine) to Savannah

(Georgia)." Since then, many post roads had been added, but carriage was still much the same: "on the public post-roads, a rider for every twenty-five or thirty miles, whose business it shall be, to proceed through his stage three times in every week, setting out immediately on receipt of the mail, and travelling with the same, by night and by day, without stopping, until he shall have delivered it to the next rider" (p. 12). As of 1820, the stages probably went from Brunswick through Gardiner and then to Jefferson. Direct postal service to Patricktown began in 1837, when the Patricktown post office was established. With a few short interruptions, the post office continued there until 1908, when it was discontinued. Now Somerville once again receives its mail through the Jefferson post office.

2. The identity of Samuel A. Kennedy and his relationship with Ephraim Kennedy remain a mystery. In this original letter, transcribed by Kathryn Gaynor, a professional genealogist, Samuel refers to Ephraim as "brother." However, it is not apparent from the genealogical record that Ephraim *had* a brother named Samuel. Ephraim's parents, John and Judith Kennedy, died in 1808 and 1809, when he was only four and five years old. John and Judy had at least six other children, but none with the first name Samuel. After his parents' death, Ephraim was raised by Sebra Crooker's brother, Frances Crooker, and his wife, Ana Mattocks Crooker. They did not have any children. Was Samuel a second name of one of his brothers? Or was Samuel merely a friend? The only record of a matching Samuel A. Kennedy in Massachusetts around 1830 is a marriage record ("Massachusetts, Marriages, 1695–1910," index, FamilySearch [https://familysearch.org/pal:/MM9.1.1/FHNW-6BS : accessed December 8, 2013], Samuel A. Kennedy and Mary P. Piper, 13 Nov 1831) of Samuel A. Kennedy marrying a Mary P. Piper in Newburyport, Massachusetts, in 1831. To make matters more confusing, there *is* a Samuel Kennedy who lived down the road from Ephraim, but he was apparently the descendant of a different Kennedy line, a Samuel Kennedy who lived in Newcastle, and probably knew Sebra Crooker, moving around the same time to Patricktown. Whatever the relationship, there was a real bond between the men, as Ephraim did indeed go on to name his first son Samuel.

3. 1830 Federal Census of Patricktown.

4. Judd, Churchill, and Eastman (eds.), *The Pine Tree State from Prehistory to the Present*, pp. 221 and 232.

5. Lydia Crooker married Rufus Boynton, and Mary Crooker married John Crooker, a relative. Both men bought land adjoining Sebra Crooker's.

6. Judd, Churchill, and Eastman (eds.), *The Pine Tree State from Prehistory to the Present*, p. 253.

7. Ibid., p. 257. In 1820, with the opening of the Eerie Canal, they could now get "Genesee Flour," milled on the Genesee River in Rochester, New York. For a time, there were so many flour mills in Rochester that it was known as "The Flour City" (http://falzguy.com/high-falls.html, accessed December 2013).

8. From an original deed from David and Leonard Fish to Ephraim Kennedy, recorded in the Lincoln County Registry of Deeds. Ephraim bought one hundred acres for $500 on March 9, 1830.

9. Ibid., p. 247.

10. http://www.ramshornstudio.com/early_lighting_7.htm. Argand lamps, developed in Switzerland in 1780, allowed for more complete combustion of liquid oils, thus creating a brighter light. Their popularity soon spread across the ocean, and local manufacturers began producing them for the American market. They remained the most popular lighting source until the 1850s, when kerosene lamps were developed.

11. Ibid., p. 257.

12. Billie Gammon and Glenda Richards, *Rural Reflections 1840s to 1880s: So You Will Know That You May Share a Way of Life Far Different Than Your Own* (Livermore, ME: Washburn-Norlands Foundation, 1978), p. 22.

13. Stavely and Fitzgerald, *America's Founding Food*, p. 26.

14. Judd, Churchill, and Eastman, *The Pine Tree State from Prehistory to the Present*, p. 257.

15. http://www.mainething.com/history/history.htm, accessed November 2013. Marie Sacks, "A History of Whitefield." Written for inclusion in the Whitefield Comprehensive Plan, and an abstract of *A Brief History of Whitefield 1760–2004*, available through the Whitefield Historical Society. The carding mill is visible on the 1857 map of North Whitefield, by C. M. Hopkins, surveyor, *A Topographical Map of Lincoln, County, Maine* (Philadelphia: C. M. Hopkins, 1857).

16. Day, *History of Maine Agriculture*, p. 119.

17. Ibid., pp. 231–32. Also see page 178: "The establishment of woolen weaving mills was initially slow, due to the competition from homespun production; early mills did carding and fulling of home-grown wool for home spinning and weaving." In William H. Bunting, *A Day's Work: A Sampler of Maine Historic Photographs, Part One* (Gardiner, ME: Tilbury House, 1997).

18. Russell, *A Long, Deep Furrow*, p. 159.

19. Allard, French, Cranmer, and Milakovsky, *Then & Now: Patricktown/Somerville. Volume Two: History*, p. 6.

20. From original deeds recorded in the Lincoln County Registry of Deeds.

21. Ibid., p. 7.

22. Ibid.

23. Ibid., p. 61; Russell, *A Long, Deep Furrow*, p. 188.

24. Day, *History of Maine Agriculture*, p. 90.

25. Ibid., p. 93.

26. Ibid., p. 88.

27. Ibid., pp. 226–30.

28. Ibid., p. 241.

29. Russell, *A Long, Deep Furrow*, p. 281.

30. Ancestry.com. *Selected U.S. Federal Census Non-Population Schedules, 1850–1880* [online database]. Provo, UT, USA: Ancestry.com Operations, Inc., 2010.

31. Judd, Churchill, and Eastman, *The Pine Tree State from Prehistory to the Present*, p. 257.

32. 1850 Federal Census of Patricktown.

33. Allard, French, Cranmer, and Milakovsky, *Then & Now: Patricktown/ Somerville. Volume Two: History*, pp. 64–98.

34. Ibid., p. 7.

November 2009
The Gift of Garlic

I HAD BRACED myself for the normal fall ritual of garlic planting, stiff fingers fumbling cloves into half-frozen soil. However, the day has turned unexpectedly warm, and I am soon hanging my hat and jacket on a fence post. The sunshine is a blessing, freeing the skies from the perpetually dismal gray that had been slowly suffocating the sun.

As I bend my way down the row, I marvel at this cold beginning, the natural rhythm that has created this planting of life among the decay of the previous year. I am always amazed, despite having seen the new shoots poking pale green from the mulch, at the revival of hope in the earliest days of spring.

Garlic was the first crop I planted as an adult, working with my friend, Beth, in her garden, excited by this foray into a new world. An occasional gardener, a creative force in her own right, she had led me to many new things, and unlike the proverbial horse, I had needed no encouragement to drink deeply.

As a tentative but determined young woman, I had grown in her company without prodding or restriction. She was possibility and excitement, believing in me before even I knew which way I was growing. She had listened well and heard the longing I scarcely recognized, the ache I scarcely dared utter. That year she awoke in me the wonder of garlic, and in the fall we combined it with the abundant basil I had carefully transplanted, unable as a novice gardener to thin without remorse. Together we created, the herbs shrinking in the blender, darkening into a sauce magical in its intensity and raw evocation of life.

Later, distracted by years of academia, I was once again led by her back to the dark earth and felt the immediate physical connection pouring through my hands. Her gift was simple, innocuous in its blandness: some extra garlic shoots she had thinned from her garden and brought wrapped in a plastic bag, "in case you want to plant them." I had not gardened for years; I was a semi-transient adult living in my parents' house with my new husband, and I was desperately trying to finish my dissertation, tied for hours to the computer, while my body and spirit withered.

The bag sat there for days, unremarked, low priority in a world of deadlines, but there nonetheless, slowly working its way into my being. Then, one sunny spring day when the chains to my desk were weakened, I walked up to my father's old garden, long overgrown with weeds, and started to make room for these small green shoots, these tenderest of garlic progeny that would take two years to bear. The weeds yielded easily, their roots only lightly held by the soft soil, and soon the borders of the garden started to emerge.

By the time I headed down the field, I was dirty and exultant, transfigured, unable to separate myself from that small but hopeful plot of earth. My center had shifted, my world expanded, and I felt it in an immediate physical way, the shifting blue vault of the sky dispelling the heavy ceiling of my room. That spring, that garlic, those moments of infinite freedom and yet deepest connection, had loosened my dreams of farming—not as a matter of study or policy, but as a way of life, immersed in the land, body, mind, and spirit. This time I would not resist. The garden expanded; I submitted my dissertation and returned with my husband to find our own farm.

This was her legacy, to me and many others—this permission to live as we were called. To let the small voice of our secret dreams pipe out; to pause, listen, and answer them back. To take up the challenge and make it work. To remember in the fulfilling that we were responsible for retaining wonder and recognizing the beauty we sought. To know in this life—our one life—the full satisfaction of ourselves in our creations.

Here I stumble, my hands seeking the steadiness of the earth, doubt replacing exultation, for now Beth's own life, so rich and generous, was suddenly uncertain. She was fighting, fighting hard, with bright spirit and gritty anger, against both breast and ovarian cancer. Yet there were no certainties in this battle, no assurance that dreams and determination would prevail.

She was buffeted, and she fought, and the world seemed less gentle for its treatment of her. Even the garlic cloves, waiting alone in the frozen soil, seemed more certain of the nurturing sun. As I mound a thick layer of compost and mulch over them, tucking them into their winter bed, I pray that spring will be kind.

November 2009

Tractor

IT IS a bleak day, uninviting, and the house seems especially warm in comparison, the reds and golds of the living room contrasting with the gray world outside. Still, I know Keiran and I would benefit from some fresh air, cold blast though it may be.

Once outside, we find the landscape illuminated by a stray light not visible from the house. Somehow evading the low-hanging clouds, the sun washes the pasture in a golden hue, transforming the bent brown grass into a sea of amber, its stiff waves frozen until spring. Goldenrod and thistle hold their flowers stalks defiantly aloft, offering their seeds to the fall wind.

A small red polar bear in his three layers, Keiran is all business, immediately heading for the barn. Finally free of my hand, he is fearless, plunging across the overgrown lawn with abandon. Only as we reach the bottom of the ramp does he take my finger, unable to navigate the slope alone. Together we lift the latch and pass through the doorway into the shadowy world of the barn.

From all corners we can hear animals stirring, unaccustomed to our presence at this hour. Our cats, Jade and Diego, greet us from on high, treading a delicate tightrope from beam to beam, while we take a more humble route to the pigpen. A few weeks before, we had bought two Tamworth piglets, a heritage breed of British origin. Descendants of the native pigs of Europe, they were supposed to be better suited to grazing than our previous conventional breeds.

I was enamored with their long, hairy, red bodies and delicate snouts, so different from the stocky, snub-nosed white piglets we had before. Rhodora, as I had named the sow, reminded me of the wild rhododendrons that grew by the brook, while Anil had named the boar Redman, in fond memory of a distant friend. The attraction, however, was definitely one-sided; so far they wanted little to do with us. This morning they lay buried in the hay at the far end of the pen, only their eyes following our movements. I call Rhodora's name, shake a little grain into the pan as enticement, then stand for a moment like a stricken admirer, content just to watch them.

The goats, suffering from no such restraint, call out in impatience, and I direct Keiran back to our curious herd. The goats press up to the fence, hopeful, and Keiran forgets his fears. "Maaa," he says, "maaa," and reaches for the goats. As I break a bale into wedges, filling the feeders, he bounces in place, holding onto the fence with both hands.

The Saanens ignore him, focused on the sweet-smelling hay, but our Nubian is skittish, backing away from this bundle of noise and commotion. Her kids shadow her, finding places at the farthest hayrack. All settle to business until one of the goats snorts, a short, sharp burst of air that sounds ridiculously like a fart, and Keiran explodes in laughter. Mimic that he is, he snorts back, exploring the range of possible tones. This is too much for the goats, and the pen becomes a whirlwind of moving bodies, seeking escape from their littlest caretaker. Perhaps an ignominious beginning to Keiran's days as farmhand, but for me the day is illuminated.

As I steer Keiran out the barn door, I hear the *bub–bub–bub–bub* of Don's tractor starting up across the road. Unlike the businesslike drone of the newer tractors, the old John Deere has a more expressive voice, a repetitive sputter as if perpetually surprised to still be alive.

In gradual concession to his age, Don has been slowly selling off his tractors, putting them through their paces for prospective buyers.

Although we desperately needed a tractor, we wanted one with a bucket, and the old tractors were not made for such attachments. Relegated to the sidelines, we tried to ignore our sense of loss at their eventual departure, for Don himself admitted no such sentiment. But the memories were there: in the ease with which he mounted them, one long leg lifting him up to the humming seat, and the speed with which he drove them into the low-ceilinged shed.

Today, however, there are no buyers appraising the tractors with dispassionate eyes. Work has called them forth, the man and the machine, joined once again in purpose. The engine hums energetically, and Don moves quickly, loading his chainsaw on the wagon. He hasn't seen me, and I stand watching him in unabashed awe, amazed to see him heading off to cut firewood.

At eighty-seven, his limits must encroach upon his freedom daily, yet he moves with confidence and a slightly stiff grace, drawing on the strength and skill he has forged in a lifetime of self-reliance. As he straightens to mount the tractor, he spots us and waves in silent greeting. Despite the short distance between us, the engine drowns any thought of conversation, so he heads our way, leaving the tractor vibrating in idle like an impatient horse.

I would go to meet him, but Keiran is frozen at my side, grasping my finger, every particle of his being focused and fascinated. Around the age of ten months, he had developed a singular fascination with all things motorized, surprising me one day with a very realistic *brrmmm, brrmmm.*

Having no mechanical inclinations myself, I had not anticipated his sudden fanatical obsession. His vocabulary of animal sounds was easily explained, surrounded as he was by livestock noisily demanding attention. But his attraction to trucks and diggers was all his own, springing from some secret well that I could not fathom. I was both perplexed and enchanted, feeling the full mystery of his separate soul, wondering what other passions trembled for release.

Happily, his devotion to machinery had coincided with the beginning of the haying season, and for weeks tractors were busy in the surrounding fields: mowing, tedding (turning), baling. The sudden hum and rattle as the tractors sprang to life, their attachments busily turning behind them, unfailingly penetrated Keiran's world. *Rac, rac* he would cry, abandoning all else in pursuit of the siren machine.

In the cool of the evening, we would walk through the fields to the silent machines, their large bodies like slumbering elephants, concealing their power. With awkward determination, I would scale their sides, Keiran tucked precariously next to me. Pulling with one hand, pushing with one foot, we would somehow settle into our high perch. The fields looked different from this vantage point, and I was free to relax and admire, while Keiran busily directed the tractors on a mission of his own, turning the wheel and shaking the gearshift.

But now the tractor lives and breathes on its own, humming with purpose, and Keiran is spellbound, no longer the director but a breathless admirer. Don bridges the short gap between us and smiles at me but addresses his question to Keiran, farmer to farmer.

"Would you like to drive the tractor?" he asks, but there is no reply from my small son, only rapt focus.

His legs frozen, I carry him over, unprotesting, the noise enveloping us as we approach. Don points out the easiest way to slip Keiran up to the wheel, and I hoist him to the trembling seat. My hands around his waist, he sits there silently, not moving, so I turn the wheel for him in encouragement.

Don watches, then turns to me. "It's a bit much, isn't it?" he asks, but I know Keiran is fine, as he does not suffer silently.

We are all three quiet for a while, happy captives to the roaring tractor. Gradually Keiran comes to life, his muscles released, and he bends cautiously forward to explore. The knobs and levers jump and startle under his hand like a nervous pony, but he guides his steed with increasing confidence. When he finally straightens, I lift him from the seat, bringing him back to the ground and his unsteady toddler legs.

As I wave our thanks, Don also is released, and all is motion again, the tractor responding instantly to its master's commands. He spins a tight circle in the road, backs expertly into the wagon's hitch, and drives into the field, heading for the tree line.

As the tractor's engine fades into the forest, I hear the familiar *brrmmm, brrmmm* of Keiran's engine revving into life, their connection undimmed by distance.

November 2009

Generations

AS FALL draws to a close, we free ourselves from farm duties for a trip to the city to check the status of my pregnancy. Now an inseparable family of four, we troop in to the shadowy room, eager to view our newest member. As the technologist passes her wand across my belly, probing the mysteries within, Anil directs Keiran's attention to the screen above our heads.

Almost immediately the technologist laughs. "You're having a girl!" she says, sharing in our delight. She interprets the shadowy image for us, clarifying the unmistakably feminine parts. Looking at the screen with some disbelief, my own feelings are suspended, the blurred photo less real than the unmistakable tapping within.

My daughter. It is only later, on the phone discussing "when she is born," that I hear *she* echoing in my mind, trickling bit by bit to my soul. A daughter. There is something strangely mortal in that pronouncement, as if my own life span has suddenly been set. My son, my son so beloved, is no less flesh of my flesh, spark of my soul. And yet it is this image of a little girl, growing through childhood into womanhood, which makes me feel myself passing on. All the dreams and fears, the realities of womanhood, will now be hers. I am suddenly one of those faded generations, those caretakers of the land who have loved and moved on, leaving their legacy in stone walls and beams, in pastures and hawthorn trees.

What do we do? What do any of us do? We walk a little in the sun, we sing and cry and shout in anger and exuberance, then we fade back, more or less gently, into the shadow of the trees. We plant seeds each spring for the promise of the ripened tomato, the delicately sweet string bean, the decadent, golden-fleshed squash. We cook for our children, as if we could fortify their bodies against pain and loss. We carry them in our arms, and for that brief moment we are the world. We cry and fight and make love with such passion, as if this was It, this was The Moment.

And yet we fade away, fade away, generation after generation, and only the sun is still there, rising over the hills, warm and relentless, and the darkness of night, made blacker by the tiny prickles of stars. From our vantage point on Hewett Road, surrounded by forest and fields, the night sky looks bigger, darker, and more brilliant than any I have seen. The Milky Way is a river of light, a city of stars, with more depth than I had ever imagined. It almost hurts to look, to focus for a minute on an individual speck, shimmering out its life. Death is all around us: that moment of parting, of shifting, the ripping out of life's seams and sinking into eternity's unbounded embrace. Where do we go? I suppose where we came from, wherever that may be.

In the face of such immensity, it is these small daily activities that seem of utmost importance. What more is there than to live carefully, in good relationship? In the preparing of food, we draw close to the earth, we draw life from the earth, and in turn we nourish our families and friends. Sharing in the small busyness of a child, discovering stones and dried leaves, we expose ourselves to eternity.

Birth and death demand our attention, the transformations reminding us of the tenuous place we all hold, the finite within the infinite embrace. But the infinite is no less present in between, in the quiet moments of growth, and here we are richly rewarded as farmers. We pause, hoe or pitchfork in hand, looking out over field or stock, resting our souls as much as our bodies. If we but notice these smallest of moments, do we not gain eternity?

PART II

WINTER:
STAYING THE COURSE

1874

Francis and Calista Kennedy

THE ROAD is broad now and well kept, the gravel hard-packed from the weight of passing wagons. Today, however, the lone wagon on the road moves slowly, and though it is loaded with passengers, it is strangely silent. The horse alone moves with purpose, the muffled clopping of its hooves in rhythmic counterpoint to the creaking of the wagon.

The shrill cry of an infant shatters the precarious peace, its insistent cries rippling out into the quiet. At the reins, Francis Kennedy, thirty-two years old, in the somber gray of mourning, turns to look back at his children, huddled together along the narrow rear bench. His eldest daughter, Julia, holds the fussing baby, while six-year-old Edith, already responsible, bends over him, offering a bottle. Francis frowns in concern as the baby turns his head, evading the unfamiliar nipple. Only six weeks old, his tiny son, John Erwin, was already motherless, and he looked vulnerable in his sister's arms, a burden too big for her age.

With a sudden sense of urgency, he turns back to the horse, urging it on, impatient to get his children home. But as the horse trots past the one-room schoolhouse and the neighbors' farms, as their own pretty house comes into view, he slows again, suddenly reluctant to enter, to accept this new life without Calista. Calista, his beloved wife, was only twenty-seven years old, full of energy and laughter, but death had taken her anyway, and life seemed quiet and still without her.

They had married in 1864, shortly after his mother Julia had died, and Calista, only seventeen, had poured her youthful energy into their home and growing family. With so much to do, the ten years of their marriage had sped by in a whirlwind of work. They had added another room on the house and a fine porch, and when they sat in the evening, they had dreamed of their future together.

Now, for the second time, he had lost the most important woman in his life, and he and Ephraim were on their own once more. Alone, he thought, with five children. As they crowd around him at the door of the house, he wonders how he will manage without her. Ephraim was a huge support, but, at seventy, his father knew little more of child care than he did.

Like most of the residents of Somerville, they were farmers, and they needed to be out in the barn and fields, not inside tending children. He had enough to worry about with his flock of sheep, scarcely enough time to cut hay for the winter. Julia and Edith, at eight and six, could already help around the house, and little Frank, only four years old, was more eager to help him than some men he knew. Still, they were too young to be left in charge of toddler Violet and baby John.

Changing into his work clothes, he watches their serious faces, unsure of themselves without their mother's guidance. Suddenly he knows that he cannot leave them, so he motions for them to follow him, turning with some relief out of the house. Grateful not to be left behind, they hurry after him like a bunch of small chicks and pile back in the wagon.

The late September grass is sweet but sparse, and the sheep have eaten down the near fields. When they see Francis, they call to him in deep and resonant unison. They run along the fence line, baa-ing, as the wagon trundles down to the brook. Loosening the horse's reins, he leaves it to drink while he heads over to the fence.

Opening the gate, he steps aside as the sheep push past, impatient for fresh pasture. At the water's edge they pause, but soon an older ewe finds the stone bridge and heads across the brook, the others in single file behind. Soon a narrow line of puffy white spans the blue river, and he smiles to see them spilling out onto the far green field. Immediately they set to grazing, heads down, drifting up the hill like lazy summer clouds.

He had begun clearing the back hills when he decided to raise sheep commercially, knowing they would soon exhaust the near pasture. To reach the far hills, he had to drive his ox team across the brook, a tricky job in the spring melt or summer rains, when water and mud impeded their passage. In an ingenious feat of engineering, he had built a wide, stone bridge, inspired by the wealth of rock he harvested from the fields every spring.

With the patient assistance of his oxen, he had hauled large rocks into the stream, leaving room for water to flow between them. He then placed large, flat rocks over the boulders and covered all with smaller rocks and dirt. Now, four years later, he surveyed his stonework with satisfaction; it had worked remarkably well. The bridge, only a few feet above the riverbed, was dry most of the year and provided adequate traction even when flooded. It had been so successful that he had later constructed the narrower footpath for the sheep.

Driving the team across the bridge, he and Ephraim set to work cutting the tall grass, their scythes swinging in counterpoint. It would not be long before the frost burned the grass, and they still needed a lot of hay to feed the stock through the winter. His mind circling from the past to the future, he looks up, suddenly shaken, reminded of the present. Relieved, he sees the children gathering herbs along the edge of the field, the baby safely swaddled.

He and Ephraim had pushed back the woods little by little, felling trees, clearing rocks, stumping and plowing. It was not work that could be rushed, but every year they gained a little ground. Thankfully, the oxen were as patient as they, and he was rewarded by the sight of the grass waving green across the hills.

He and his father had worked together to build a fine and prosperous farm, and their family had little want. Although wool prices had dropped sharply since the war had ended in 1865, wool had fluctuated several times in the decades before the war, so he had decided to stay the course, hoping that prices would recover with the economy. Surely the formation of the United States Department of Agriculture in 1862[1] meant that the government was behind farmers. Conservative but hopeful, like most farmers, Francis trusted that the land and hard work would provide for his family.

Francis had been born in the golden era[2] of New England sheep farming, when the growing textile industry had raised wool prices to their highest level ever. His father, first and foremost a homesteader, had not been seduced into the craze for Merinos with their fine but light fleece. Instead, he had stuck with the native sheep, hardy, dual-purpose animals good for both meat and wool. Their coarser fleece was fine for homespun, and its heavier total weight compensated for its lower price.

The growing demand for both mutton and wool and the ease of railroad access had inspired Ephraim to build up his flock, and, in the war years, his choice had seemed good. Between 1861 and 1864, the price of wool had leaped from 33 cents a pound to 73 cents.[3] With cotton no longer coming up from the South, there was a huge demand for all grades of wool to meet the army's needs for uniforms and blankets.[4]

Although almost a quarter of Somerville's men—72 out of 325—went to fight in the Civil War, Francis had stayed home to help on the farm. Most of his brothers and sisters had married and moved out, but he had a special bond with his mother, and he enjoyed farm life. However, while he could evade the army, he could not so easily dissuade death, and his inevitable separation from his mother was not long delayed. On June 5, 1864, at fifty-five years of age, Julia passed on, leaving behind her husband and son.

Suddenly anchorless, Francis reached out for stability, and Calista Chadwick, then seventeen years old, took his hand and steadied him. They married the day after Christmas, setting up house with his father, and all the responsibilities of the household settled on her young shoulders. With Ephraim's assistance, they expanded the house, adding a few rooms to accommodate their growing family. When, a year later, Calista gave birth to a young daughter, they named her Julia, filling the house with his mother's name once again.

After the war, things hadn't seemed so promising for him or for Somerville. As cotton once more flooded the mills, the price of wool began a steep decline, while the prices of goods remained inflated. Other Somerville farms faced more personal—and debilitating—losses: Of the seventy-two men who had gone off to war, sixteen never returned, and six were now disabled.[5]

Many of those who did return were too restless to settle down again. Children of settlers, they had grown up with the expectation of a small-town life, most likely in farming or a local trade. Traveling with the army, however, they had seen cities and farms of all types: larger, flatter, with deeper, more fertile soil.

In comparison, the small, stony farms of Somerville seemed less of an opportunity and more of a lifetime sentence. The woodlots that had sustained many of the hillier farms had been cut down, and the farms struggled to compete with cheaper Western grain and wool. To add insult to injury, farm property taxes had hit a new high, reaching $0.006 in 1870, compared to $0.002 before the war.[6]

Suddenly, the 160 acres of Western land promised by the Homestead Acts of 1862 and 1864 seemed a promising alternative,[7] even if it meant starting over—and this generation still had the necessary skills to be pioneers. For women, too, there were new opportunities, as the booming mill industry was eager to hire female labor. Across Maine, small towns started to decline, and Somerville's population decreased to 506 in 1870.[8]

Looking across the river to the house and barn, Francis was thankful for the piece of land he had inherited. This was his home; he had not chosen to leave it before, and he did not plan to leave it now. Perhaps it could not compare to the vast prairie farms out West, but it had supported his family for two generations, and he had not failed in its upkeep. Every spring he spread the winter's manure on a different field, and he could always see the difference in the grass. Likewise in the forest, as he carefully selected trees to harvest, he noticed old cuts filling in, assuring him of next year's harvest. Usually he cut about twenty cords a year, earning a substantial $40.[9] If he cared for the land, it seemed, the land would care for him—and his family.

Although the sheep's wool, about sixty pounds a year, was mostly destined for the market, he had always, first and foremost, provided for household needs. The vagaries of weather were unavoidable, but he would not subject his family or farm to the fickleness of the market. The collapse of the financial markets in the Panic of 1873[10] had caused farm prices to drop rapidly; butter had fallen from 38 cents a pound in 1866 to 26 cents in 1873.[11] While he needed cash for taxes and an increasing amount of farm inputs, his parents and grandparents had survived by barter and trade, and he knew how to put food directly on the table.

To accommodate his growing flock of sheep, almost twenty, counting the lambs,[12] he had built an addition on the barn, with hay storage overhead. The bulk of the barn, however, was still filled with the stock that fed the family. The girls' flock of chickens had grown to twenty, and the single milk cow produced about a hundred pounds of butter—enough to last through the winter, and have surplus to barter at the country store. Many farmers were switching to horses for all their draft needs, but he still kept a pair of oxen for the hard work of plowing. Although, as some observed, oxen had only two speeds, "slow and slower," he had remedied this somewhat by hitching them behind a horse.[13]

With wheat flour so readily available, he no longer grew rye, and only half as much Indian corn (thirty bushels) as his father had. Still, with sixty-five bushels of oats and eight bushels of beans, there was plenty to thresh in the winter. The cellar was already filled with a hundred bushels of potatoes, and the apple trees promised another eighty bushels or so, much of which he would sell to eager neighbors, earning a welcome $20. Still, the greatest portion of his land was used for the sweetly redolent hay—about twenty tons a year[14]—that fed ox and cow, horse and sheep, through the long months of winter.

Surveying the long line of cut grass that stretched behind him, he paused, resting his scythe on the ground with a sigh. It would have to be enough; the children would need food—and rest. Hopefully it would not rain. Tomorrow they would return to shake up the hay with long tedding sticks, fluffing and turning it so that it would dry quickly.[15] Signaling to Ephraim and the children, he walked back to the wagon, suddenly tired.

When darkness finally falls, the children sleep, but Francis sits on the bed, unable to rest in its strange emptiness. Needing an outlet for his energy, he heads to the cooper shop, glad to keep his hands busy. With so many lime kilns in the area, there was always a demand for barrels—lime casks, as they were known in the trade. New York City alone had a seemingly inexhaustible appetite for lime, and the kilns in Rockland bought hundreds of thousands of barrels a year.[16]

Securing a fresh plank in the jaws of the shaving horse,[17] he sat on the other end, keeping his foot pressed against the pedal. Carefully, he ran his long drawknife up the wood, curving it so that the tops and bottoms would be narrower than the middle.[18] The finished staves had to fit together perfectly, as wet lime would swell and burn, endangering the boats—and crew—en route to New York.

Intent on the steady rhythm of his task, he barely notices the dark hours of night slipping by or the pile of shaped staves rising next to him. Only the light of dawn draws him away, back into the world, to face its unavoidable reality. Slowly straightening, he surveys his work; he will light the fire and bend the staves another day, then bind them with the long hoops that are drying in the barn. Now he knows the children will soon be stirring, and heads back into the house.

Confronting dawn out his window, he pauses to look at the young hawthorn stretching its thorny fingers to the lightening sky. He had brought the tree home on the train from Hingham, Massachusetts, when he went to visit his sister, Sylvia. Christian tradition tied the hawthorn to purity and spiritual growth, and, like Joseph of Arimathea, he had planted it as a sign of his faith. But when he showed Ephraim, his father had laughed, recounting the legends of his Irish family, who believed that it was an entrance to the fairy world. They had planted it near the house, and if fairies dwelt in its branches, they were at peace with their Christian neighbors.

Every May it had bloomed, rightfully earning its name of May-tree, and Calista had delighted in the small white flowers which transformed its thorny branches into a bridal veil. Remembering his own radiant bride, Francis bends his head. He is a man of faith, and he prays, seeking solace in the words he had inscribed on her stone: *We long for household*

*voices gone, For vanished smiles we long, But God hath led our dear ones on,
And he can do no wrong.*

The years ahead were to be hard ones, and Francis would need his faith to see him through. The next spring, March 14, 1875, at seven months old, baby John finally gave up his struggle to live. With the loving persistence of his family, he had survived the long winter, but, weakened without his mother's milk, he finally followed her beyond mortal confines.

It was the beginning of a long, dark period, as Maine—indeed, all of New England—headed into an even more difficult time for agriculture. The thirty years from 1870 to 1900 were "decades of almost unrelieved gloom."[19] Prices continued to slump. By 1879 butter was 14 cents a pound,[20] but taxes remained high, and farms continued to be abandoned.

In an effort to help its cash-strapped citizens, the town of Somerville voted in 1881 to allow residents to work out their tax in road maintenance, at the rate of 20 cents an hour for men and oxen.[21] Portable sawmills replaced the older, water-powered ones, chasing the receding line of trees further into the forest. An abundance of hemlock bark fueled a brief tannery boom in Somerville,[22] and many farmers grew cannery beans for processors in nearby Liberty.[23]

Farmers, used to enduring, remained hopeful, but by 1880 Maine had reached its pinnacle of farm development.[24] The 64,000 farms in 1880 would decline to 59,000 by 1900, a downward trend that has continued to this day.[25] Despite its best efforts, Somerville lost farms as well, their number shrinking from 96 in 1880 to 70 in 1900.[26]

Those were the "lean and hungry years," and "determination and real ability were required to make a good living and educate a family on many a Maine farm . . ."[27] For the twice-motherless Kennedy family, there was the added burden of personal loss; somehow they had to function as a womanless family at a time when every hand was needed.

In such times of need, it was often the farm woman who made up the immediate shortfalls, by producing or saving a little more. In this case, the women of the household were only girls, but they already knew their basic trades.[28] Butter and eggs were always good barter at the general store, and canning helped to extend the garden's bounty into the winter. Since the development of the Mason jar in 1858, home canning had made it relatively easy to safely preserve vegetables, fruit, and even meat.[29] As Edith was to record in her cookbook years later, this was a trade she learned young.

CORN

The corn must be fresh. Husk, remove the silk, cut from cob, and pack in sterilized jars. Adjust new rubbers, put tops on loosely, and place jars in the boiler on a rack. Fill the boiler with cold water, place on the fire, and boil for 1½ hours. Screw on top tight. Boil for another hour, remove from the water, and before putting away, be sure the tops are tight. Better add 1 teaspoon salt to each jar.

A grandfather, a father, and a pack of children—together, somehow, they made do, in the leanest of years, when many other family farms gave up the struggle. Perhaps the secret of their survival is also in Edith's cookbook, recorded years later for her own daughter:

PAPA'S COOKIES

One cup of molasses, one cup of sugar, two-thirds cup of lard, one large teaspoon soda dissolved in one tablespoonful of hot water, salt, cassia or ginger or lemon, is very nice; mix very stiff (with flour) and bake quickly.

GRANDPA'S COOKIES

One cup sour cream, one cup sugar, one teaspoon soda, one teaspoon cream of tartar, a little salt and nutmeg. Flour enough to make a soft dough, or leave out the cream of tartar and use one egg.

It is easy to imagine her, a girl making cookies to delight the hearts and mouths of those she loved. A girl with responsibilities beyond her years, blending a child's delight—in cookies!—with a woman's compassionate care. Perhaps the recipe is love.

NOTES

1. Russell, *A Long, Deep Furrow*, p. 281.
2. Day, *History of Maine Agriculture*, p. 187.

3. Clarence Albert Day, *Farming in Maine 1860–1940* (Orono: University of Maine Press, 1963), p. 19.

4. Russell, *A Long, Deep Furrow*, p. 251.

5. Allard, French, Cranmer, and Milakovsky, *Then & Now: Patricktown/ Somerville. Volume Two: History*, p. 19.

6. Russell, *A Long, Deep Furrow*, p. 257.

7. Ibid., p. 245.

8. Ancestry.com. *1870 United States Federal Census* [online database]. Provo, UT, USA: Ancestry.com Operations, Inc., 2009. Images reproduced by FamilySearch.

9. Ancestry.com. *Selected U.S. Federal Census Non-Population Schedules, 1850– 1880* [online database]. Provo, UT, USA: Ancestry.com Operations, Inc., 2010.

10. http://en.wikipedia.org/wiki/Panic_of_1873.

11. Day, *Farming in Maine*, p. 51.

12. Ancestry.com. *Selected U.S. Federal Census Non-Population Schedules, 1850–1880.*

13. Bunting, *A Day's Work*, p. 30.

14. Ancestry.com. *Selected U.S. Federal Census Non-Population Schedules, 1850–1880.*

15. Day, *History of Maine Agriculture*, p. 136.

16. Russell, *A Long, Deep Furrow*, pp. 281 and 327.

17. Bobbie Kalman, *Tools and Gadgets* (New York: Crabtree Publishing Co., 1992), p. 21.

18. Bobbie Kalman, *Visiting a Village* (New York: Crabtree Publishing Co., 1990), p. 21.

19. Russell, *A Long, Deep Furrow*, p. 256.

20. Day, *Farming in Maine*, p. 51.

21. Allard, French, Cranmer, and Milakovsky, *Then & Now: Patricktown/ Somerville. Volume Two: History*, p. 61.

22. Ibid., p. 9.

23. Ibid., p. 43.

24. Day, *Farming in Maine*, p. 18.

25. 39,000 in 1940; 6,800 in 1975.

26. Ancestry.com. *Selected U.S. Federal Census Non-Population Schedules, 1850–1880*; Ancestry.com. *1900 United States Federal Census* [online database]. Provo, UT, USA: Ancestry.com Operations, Inc., 2009. Images reproduced by FamilySearch.

27. Day, *Farming in Maine*, p. 46.

28. Russell, *A Long, Deep Furrow*, p. 288.

29. http://rcfsi.blogspot.com/2009/09/quick-history-of-home-canning.html.

December 2009

Farm Boy

E ARLY DECEMBER and still no snow. The soft, bare ground is flecked with green, and the nighttime temperatures bounce around 35, as if repelled by the freezing point. Anil predicts a warm, dry winter, but I know the plunge into darkness and cold will soon be absolute. Winter is as much a certainty as the baby in my belly, and I know we must make the passage to reach the new life waiting with the spring.

Although the cold and snow remain evasive, the darkness of winter has already descended, blacking out any thought of the sun by 4:30 p.m. Every day the darkness collects itself earlier, the shadows running together from grayness into black. Then it is time to pull the heavy curtains like erasers across the board, redrawing the room in small, cozy islands of light.

With night falling so early, Anil arrives home in the dark, his headlights burrowing through the blackness to reach our house. Keiran waits for him by the kitchen door, listening while he takes off his boots in the mudroom. Anil enters quickly, shutting the door against the rush of cold.

"There is a beautiful moon out tonight," he tells Keiran, lifting him high in the air.

"Moo," Keiran responds in delight, the "n" lost in the depths of his throat. He wiggles in protest as Anil sets him down, mournfully repeating "Moo, moo."

We had first pointed out the moon in mid-autumn, when it hung in the twilight sky like a faint scimitar. Fascinated, he had watched over his shoulder as we carried him inside. Since then, he had been searching for the moon in both sky and books, learning to recognize its changing shape. He was single-minded in his pursuit, and we were pleased with his interest in the natural world.

Indulgently we bundle him in a thick fleece blanket, wrapping it around his head and neck, only his black eyes visible. He snuggles in Anil's arms, excited, and they duck back into the cold night. They do not have far to go; just beyond the house the pasture slopes down to the brook, and the rolling expanse of fields frames the night sky. The moon is full and low, a huge, golden ball resting on the dark tree line, and Keiran nestles into Anil, a soft bundle more blanket than boy, watching.

When they return to the bright warmth of the kitchen, Keiran shadows Anil as he brings in his barn clothes to warm up. We look at each other, shrug our shoulders. It is still early; what can it hurt?

So out Keiran goes again, this time to do chores. Hand in hand, father and son navigate through the night, their flashlight carving a small tunnel to the dark bulk of the barn. Inside, Anil flips on the lights, and the barn is once again familiar, each pen a warm island of light, the animals rustling and calling for food.

While Anil fills feeders and changes water, Keiran is busy with his own tasks. Finding an old bucket, he fills it with loose hay and drags it with awkward determination to the goats' pen. On tiptoe, he reaches over the rail and drops hay onto the floor, "feeding" the goats. The cats, unused to his presence at night, drop from the rafters to investigate. Delighted to have their attention, he stops to pat them, holding his hands stiffly, mindful of our orders to "Be gentle."

The pigpen he regards with somewhat more consternation, but when Anil enters, he follows, his fascination outweighing his fear. The pigs are bigger now and much bolder, and they dash around him when he enters, their hooves clattering on the wooden floor. Holding on to the feeder for support, he stands frozen, only his dark eyes following their erratic advances and retreats.

Alone in the suddenly quiet house, I have an unexpected gift of free time, and hesitate only to decide which task to address first. Quickly lost in thought, I am unaware of time passing until I hear Keiran's bright voice punctuating the soft rhythm of Anil's speech. I turn my head in time to catch their entry, two figures now, large and small, the smell of the barn lingering on their coats. Fresh from the cold, Keiran's cheeks are rosy beacons, his eyes shining with life.

As I rise to meet them, Mommy once again, I am struck by his confidence and independence. Perhaps I had not noticed, or perhaps he has emerged from the dark night a new boy, but he is no longer a baby, following our lead, but a child with interests of his own. A small boy, yes, but one who can go off into the night and navigate its unfamiliar corners.

Nor does he forget the possibilities of this new world of darkness. The next day he turns to me, inquiring, "Moo?" Impatiently, he waits for Anil's return, and I wait with him, watching my child take his place in the life of the farm.

DECEMBER 2009
LET SLEEPING PIGS LIE

WITH NIGHT descending so early, Anil and I have time to relax in the evening. It is a luxury we never have in the long, sunlit days of summer, when garden and field beckon endlessly. Now we revel in the quiet intimacy of our home, permitted by nightfall to draw close. Many evenings we cook together, chopping and stirring to some tropical rhythm until I beg Anil for a dance. As I slide into his arms, my belly fills the space between us, but my feet briefly forget the extra weight of my unborn daughter. Only the rumblings of our combined hunger draw me back to the task at hand, the bowl of pork marinating on the counter.

Anil had not had time to cut the meat into smaller pieces, so, eager to try our own harvest, I had taken matters into my own inexperienced hands. With more than a little courage, I had selected a lumpy package marked STEW MEAT from the freezer. As it thawed, the bowl filled with surprisingly bright red blood, and the meat, softening, separated into cuts of all different sizes. Surveying my options, I was somewhat dismayed. The small pieces seemed practically all bone, while the larger chunks still had skin attached.

With only one way forward, I tackled it one piece at a time, paring away the bone and skin, slicing the meat into long strips. The process seemed messy and inexact, but as the meat emerged, cleaned and fashioned into recognizable pieces, I gained courage. Not knowing what shape of meat would emerge from my endeavors, I had selected a forgiving, bound-to-be-delicious recipe: Jamaican jerk pork. Slipping the cleaned pieces into the pungent marinade, I was at once proud and excited.

Jerk pork, one of Jamaica's culinary gifts to the world, had originated out of necessity. In the 1800s, runaway African slaves, known as Maroons, fled to the mountainous interior of Jamaica, where they survived by hunting wild hogs. The meat, seasoned with pepper and pimento berries (allspice), was spread on a wooden platform and slow-cooked over a small fire. Given the heat and moisture of the tropics, the meat had to be dried into a tough jerky if it was to be successfully preserved.

Nowadays the meat is grilled only to succulence, but the pimento and pepper marinade—at once sweet, spicy, and smoky—has become a staple of Jamaican cuisine, to the delight of locals and tourists alike. Despite having a deceptively simple list of ingredients—scallions, scotch bonnet peppers, salt, black pepper, allspice, nutmeg, cane sugar, and thyme—the true concoction of the marinade seemed to rest in Jamaican hands, and I had given up trying to make my own.

Luckily for the rest of the world, the small Jamaican village of Walkerswood had formed a community-based company and, in the 1980s, began exporting its magic. Perhaps it was their origins as a cooperative or their links to small local farmers,[1] but their seasoning was—almost— enough to transport us from the cold, dark winter to the light and heat of the islands. Combined with our pork, it was, like our family, a medley of tropical and temperate, of cultures and cuisines.

After putting the meat to slow cook in the oven, we sit on the couch and browse pork recipes, plotting a succulent course through the winter. The hours are sweet and rich, a pocket of personal delight in the busyness of farm life and parenthood. There are projects we could work on, paperwork and planning, but in these early days of winter we are reluctant to let go of this time of deep relaxation. The seed catalogs start to arrive, their pages rustling with the promise of spring and growth, but even they cannot break the sweet stupor of the winter dark.

We read, we talk, the hours stretch and contract, but inevitably the darkness wins, and we find ourselves staring at the full pages of our books with blank minds. Sleep calls sweetly, enticingly, promising the darkness of a cave and the comfort of a nest. I resist, still clock-bound, stranded from sleep by the early hour, but Anil answers the dark with gladness, pulling me behind him, a small skiff bound to his strong tides.

The first year of our marriage I had fought the current, considering sleep an obstacle to progress. The long dark nights of winter were a challenge to conquer with light and noise. "Sleep," Anil told me, his body still attuned to the unvarying rhythm of the tropical night, "sleep while you have the chance." In the summer, he reminded me, we went to bed late, coming inside only when darkness made work impossible, our eyes unable to distinguish hands from tools. Now we should rest; in fact, given icy roads and snowstorms, he argued for a societal boycott of work. We should all stay home until spring.

I listen to him with laughter and some frustration. Hard as it is to stay awake in the dark, it is harder still to fight sleep alone, when I know he is blissfully snuggled in bed. My body longs to be persuaded, but my mind revolts against his easy surrender. What could my tropical husband know of surviving a cold northern winter? I, the Yankee, will have to show him . . . tomorrow.

The very next day, browsing a magazine, I come across a reference to an article entitled "The Big Sleep," which describes human hibernation. I find the original article quickly on the Internet, in, to my surprise, the *New York Times*. On November 25, 2007, Graham Robb had submitted to the general public that "there has never been a better time to stay in bed."

While humorous in intent, it described a traditional period of winter repose on farms and rural villages across Europe. "As soon as the weather turned cold, people all over France shut themselves away and practiced the forgotten art of doing nothing at all for months on end . . . 'Seven months of winter, five months of hell,' they said in the Alps. When the 'hell' of unremitting toil was over, the human beings settled in with their cows and pigs . . ."

In 1900, the *British Medical Journal* reported of peasants in the Pskov region in northwestern Russia: "At the first fall of snow the whole family gathers round the stove, lies down, ceases to wrestle with the problems of human existence, and quietly goes to sleep. Once a day every one wakes up to eat a piece of hard bread . . . The members of the family take it in turn to watch and keep the fire alight. After six months of this reposeful existence, the family wakes up, shakes itself and goes out to see if the grass is growing."[2]

That evening I read the article to Anil, laughing, delighted despite my misgivings to find his words echoed in history. He is, as usual, right; he knows he is right; and I moderate my vehement attack on sleep. How can I resist the overwhelming force of my husband, of history, of nature itself, urging my body to sleep?

"Work will still be there tomorrow," he reminds me. "For now, sleep." Following him up the narrow stairs, I trace the quiet footsteps of earlier generations, giving in to the flow of the seasons.

NOTE

1. http://walkerswood.com/featured_farmer.php. "We utilize a network of over 1,000 individual small farmers, island-wide, to keep us supplied year-round with our fresh produce and spice requirements."

2. From the *New York Times*, November 25, 2007. © 2007 *The New York Times*. All rights reserved. Used by permission and protected by the Copyright Laws of the United States. The printing, copying, redistribution, or retransmission of this Content without express written permission is prohibited.

1895

EDITH AND WILLIAM HEWETT

A WAGON, piled high with suitcases and furniture, turns slowly onto the road. Mindful of his load, the driver, William Hewett, twenty-eight, guides the horses carefully around the ruts. Beside him, his wife, Edith, née Kennedy, twenty-seven, sits patiently, relieved to finally be going home. It is one-year-old Lloyd, safe on Edith's lap, who looks eagerly around at the tall trees and waving grass. It is a far cry from the world he has known in Philadelphia, with its paved roads and high buildings, and he holds tightly to his mother's hand in a mixture of wonder and fear.

For Edith, too, the road seems strange after her years of absence. The woods and fields are as familiar and beloved as her own skin, and yet her eyes see things differently. So much has changed for her: She is now a wife and mother, and she has lived the city life, so different a world from the farm where she grew up.

Now, though, she sighs in love and grief and anticipation; now, she— *they*, she corrects herself—are going home. She hopes William will like it here, will be able to make the transition to country life and exchange his medical work for the more settled life of farming. With his great generosity of spirit, he has given up all he has known, all he has built, so that they could return here to her birthplace. For her father needs her, needs them . . .

Lloyd points at the low, white farmhouse, and she smiles and nods—yes, that is their house! And there, there—her heart leaps in joy and grief—is her father, Francis, standing tall and slim and alone, so alone. For they have come home in the wake of loss, to fill the house once again with family and life.

When she had moved to Philadelphia, Grandpa and Frank were still at home. But Ephraim had died in 1891, and Frank, little brother Frank, had died of tuberculosis in 1893. A hopeful young son, he had kept Francis busy with plans for the farm. Now Frank too was gone, and, for the first time, she saw her father standing alone, suddenly frail. He had always seemed an iron fortress, and she had never doubted his strength—or his love.

From a young age, she had stood beside him as a helpmate, taking the place of her deceased mother. She had not played much as a child—indeed, some thought she had no play in her—but William had seen the gentleness and warmth beneath her stiff exterior.

She sighed, remembering the years of work on the farm, the responsibility of being a farm woman. For a few years she had left that behind, exchanging the countryside for the convenience of the city. But being a new mother had been lonely and confining, alone all day in their apartment while William was at work.

Now she looked with relief at the fields she knew so well. She had explored every corner while she was a child, and now, she knew, Lloyd would find endless delight in his own excursions. It was a good place for a child, she thought—for children and family—and she placed her hand gently on her growing belly. Here they would make a home.

Watching his wife beside him, William felt his own heart rise, seeing her relax a little, her cares resting more lightly on her shoulders. She had always worked hard, always been responsible, and he had hoped to give her an easier life in the city. But her heart had always been torn, so closely was she bound to her father and this farm. When she had asked him to return home and take up the mantle of farmer, he had not needed long to decide.

It would be a new adventure, he thought, and he had always liked learning a new skill. Here he could test his hand—not on the sick bodies of patients, but on the fertile body of the earth, seeking what bounty he could draw forth. He was a man of science and technology, and he understood urban markets, but he was glad he would have Francis's years of experience to help guide him. He hoped they would work well together; at fifty-three, Francis was still a strong man, invested in the future of the farm.

He knew that Francis had sometimes struggled to keep the farm afloat, but he'd never given up, and that reassured William. Perhaps they would not become rich as farmers or have the easy lifestyle they had known in the city. But there was something in being close to the land that seemed to make excess wealth superfluous. At least there was space to breathe here, he thought.

He hoped to convince Francis to move out of the sheep business and into poultry and dairy cattle. Living in Philadelphia, he had seen firsthand the enormous hunger of the city for eggs and dairy products, and he knew that railroad access would only improve in the years to come. The Turner Center Creamery in nearby Auburn had been sending iced fresh cream to Boston via rail since 1887.[1] Hopefully Francis would be willing to make some changes . . .

Luckily for William, his vision of the future was shared by the leaders in the Maine agricultural industry. As one professor of agriculture remarked later that year, "We have seen dairying grow from small beginnings until it is now the leading farm industry in Maine."[2] Protected by the cost and difficulty of long-distance refrigerated transport, the dairy and egg industries were a safer bet for farmers frustrated by Western competition in sheep, beef, and wheat.

Since 1881 the Maine Central Railroad had been running refrigerated cars between Portland, Maine, and Boston, effectively extending the Boston "milk shed" into the interior of Maine.[3] The subsequent development of the Babcock butterfat tester and the cream separator allowed customers to receive their cream a day earlier, greatly increasing demand at a time when home refrigeration was nonexistent.[4]

However, cattle required a fairly large investment to get started, so William decided to first focus on poultry. As the sheep moved out, chickens moved in, and soon a flock of laying hens had taken up residence in the barn. The eggs, destined for the Boston market, were first driven by horse and wagon to the railroad station at Winslow's Mills, a little village north of Waldoboro.

As with dairy, eggs offered a more protected market for the Maine farmer than grain or meat. In addition, the lower cost of Western grain made chicken feed more affordable, allowing farmers to retain more of the profit. As a result, by the end of the century, the number of chickens in Maine was increasing more rapidly than the number of people.[5]

No longer relegated to backyard flocks tended by women and children, chickens, as part of the "poultry industry," were suddenly taken seriously. As creatures of importance, they no longer had to roost in trees, but were provided with comfortable coops, sometimes with glass windows, as light was reported to increase egg-laying.[6] The Maine Poultry Association, formed in 1886,[7] helped to educate farmers on advances in housing, ventilation, and feed.[8] Colleges and experiment stations began developing improved breeds, resulting in the Plymouth Rock—both barred and white—and the Rhode Island Red, still two of the region's most popular breeds.[9]

While William was busy establishing himself as a farmer, Edith was reacquainting herself with the demands of being a farm wife. On January 25, 1896, her first daughter, Alice May, was born into the cold of winter, but her family—and the newly completed Baptist Church at the end of the road—welcomed her warmly into life.

Luckily the community was strong, for that was almost all Somerville had to its name at the end of the nineteenth century. The population had declined from its high of 541 in 1880 to 373 by 1900.[10] The tough economy was reflected in the households, which, though fewer in number, were larger in size. Unlike the nuclear family of settler days, parents, in-laws, and siblings all shared the same home. Some families had taken in boarders to make money, while a few individuals had hired themselves out as live-in servants to make, and save, an income.

The economic situation was so desperate that Somerville even made headlines in the *New York Times*. On June 23, 1900, under the headline

"Maine Town for Sale," the *Times* reported: "The town of Somerville, Lincoln County, Me., is for sale to the highest bidder, and it is not expected that anyone will bid very high for the place. Somerville is hopelessly bankrupt . . . It seems to have just dried up, and it is the best example known of the decayed rural town of New England—the place of deserted mills, tumbledown houses, and abandoned farms . . ."

Although not denying its bankruptcy, the local Maine paper, the *Bowdoinham Globe*, filed a more pragmatic report, reflective of local attitudes: "With almost no income, most residents had just stopped paying taxes. Farms were seized but could not be sold, and their former owners remained in residence." Surprisingly, the community seemed cheerfully resigned to the current situation. "Asked about the tax issue, a storekeeper said only, 'Yes, they're a-sockin' it to us,' before asking the correspondent to guess the number of beans in a Mason jar for a prize basket." In conclusion, the journalist offered that while ". . . the outlook for Somerville is not cheerful, yet its people are not downcast. Not a bit of it!"[11]

Although the economy alone could not determine a family's fortunes, it was not without impact. When Edith gave birth to William Hewett Jr. on September 14, 1901, there was still rejoicing over a new life, even though he was born into a difficult world. However, unlike the three previous generations, with five, six, and seven children, Edith's third child was to be her last. Children needed food and clothes and schooling, and increasingly that required cash, which was in short supply.

Drawing on the skills she had learned as a girl, Edith saved every penny she could, "putting by" a tremendous amount of food. Corn, peas, pickles, even beef could be canned, following the recipes from *The Maine Farmer* and leavened with her own experience.

To Can Green Peas

As soon as the peas have been gathered, shell them & blanch in boiling water for from two to five minutes, depending upon the size or age of the peas. Plunge into cold water for a moment and pack immediately into the jars. Fill with boiling water, add a level teaspoonful of salt per quart, put rubber and cover in position lightly, place in the canner at once, and begin sterilization. The rapidity with which these steps are taken will have a very important bearing upon the quality of the finished product.

The above is the printed recipe.

This is the way I really did it (below), and the peas are keeping beautiful now in November:

After shelling the peas I put them on the stove in boiling water and just gave them a good scald. I had my canner prepared (a big old pail with a layer cake tin turned bottom side up in the pail), and a pan of hot water to rinse my jars and set them in while filling. I work as quickly as possible, adding peas and boiling water as I go along, pressing the peas down carefully to get the air out but not enough to mash them, and ensure there is plenty of water in the jar; then, when the jar is full, add a good teaspoonful of salt, put on the cover loosely, put in the canner, and boil three hours.

I hope you will have as good luck as I have.[12]

More accustomed to work than play, Edith often appeared stern to the outside world, but if there was discipline, there was also devotion, as is readily apparent in her cookbook. Feeding two working farmers and three active children, she balanced sustenance with sweets, looking for small ways to brighten otherwise lean years. Among pages of the practical, there were many treats, lovingly recorded as "Cookies We All Like," "Chocolate Gingerbread—Alice's Favorite," "Crybaby Cookies" (that "do not make one cry, except for more"), "Candy for Old and Young," and even, not to be wasteful, "Grammie Hewett's Pork Cake," which called for "one and one half cups fat pork chopped fine."

While Edith was stretching the family's few dollars, William was looking for ways to bring in some more. Now that his poultry business was well established, he turned to the dairy industry that had so piqued his interest. With only a few cows, it was not practical to make the daily trip to the train station that the highly perishable cream required. However, associated dairying was on the rise, and so, joining with a few neighbors, he took turns driving the fifteen miles to the railroad station in Winslow's Mills. The cream, destined for the Turner Center Creamery in Auburn, Maine, would eventually reach consumers as far south as Rhode Island.[13]

Dairy cows, faced with the heavy demands of milk production, needed improved nutrition, so William began feeding grain throughout the year. Cows also required a lot more hay, but it took a lot of hands to get hay in at the right time. With three small children, William was in desperate need of a labor-saving device. Thankful for improvements in technology, he exchanged his scythe for a horse-drawn mowing machine in the early 1900s.

As the years went by, William would increasingly have the help of science and technology to assist him in his production. Confronted with the needs of a burgeoning population, the national government became more involved in agriculture and rural affairs through both regulation and investment. In 1913 the Maine Experiment Station initiated research in "breeding and feeding problems in cattle and poultry," and the extension service started educational programs for farm boys and girls.[14]

While the government addressed the educational concerns of the next generation of farmers, it was the mothers who tended to their more delicate needs. At eighteen years old, young Lloyd Hewett was distracted by spring. If the farm was to keep him here, there would have to be more than cows to hold his interest.

As Edith recorded in her cookbook on May 14, 1912:

I made this candy . . . to put in May baskets,[15] with chocolate for Lloyd to hang at Cooper's Mills. Very nice indeed.

SEA FOAM CANDY

Two cups full of sugar—light brown of hue
a teacup of water added thereto.
Must boil until done, and this is the test:
Dropped in cold water a bit may be pressed
into soft shapes that will easily budge
(less brittle than taffy—harder than fudge).
Have ready—stiff whipped—the white of one egg,

and pour in the syrup—slowly, I beg—
all the time stirring with increasing haste,
and adding vanilla extract to taste;
then beat a while longer till, very light,
the mixture proclaims your effort just right.
Drop from your spoon's tip, with infinite care
onto pharaffine paper the candy so fair.
And each little snowy, glistening heap
will look like the foam that crowns the great deep.
The sea's children though would envy our treat—
far better, I'm sure they would find it to eat.

NOTES

1. Russell, *A Long, Deep Furrow*, p. 263.

2. Day, *Farming in Maine*, p. 53.

3. Ibid., p. 53.

4. Ibid., p. 58.

5. Russell, *A Long, Deep Furrow*, p. 267.

6. Ibid., p. 210.

7. Ibid., p. 285.

8. Ibid., p. 266.

9. Ibid., p. 268.

10. Ancestry.com. *1880 United States Federal Census* [online database]. Provo, UT, USA: Ancestry.com Operations, Inc., 2009. Images reproduced by Family-Search; Ibid., 1900.

11. Allard, French, Cranmer, and Milakovsky, *Then & Now: Patricktown/ Somerville. Volume Two: History*, p. 10.

12. Edith Hewett, unpublished, handwritten recipe book.

13. Day, *Farming in Maine*, p. 70.

14. Ibid., pp. 297 and 299.

15. May baskets were traditionally given to friends—and sweethearts—during the month of May, in hopes of a kiss.

January 2010
Here We Stay

J ANUARY ARRIVES, and with it all doubts of winter recede. The thermometer plunges toward zero with single-minded determination, and the wind rises, making a mockery of scarves and jackets. It is too cold to bring Keiran outside, so I do morning chores while he naps, hunching into my jacket, my shoulders tightening in subconscious defense.

The goats watch me without rising, reluctant to leave their own pockets of body heat. Only as I shake open the bales of hay do they stand, still hunched, and cluster around the feeders, eating without their usual loose-limbed tussle. Returning to the warm kitchen, I roll my neck, trying to shake off the stress of the cold. Even in the house, winter is present, rattling shutters, slamming doors, growling in frustration as she seeks entry.

If this is the reality of winter, it is a reality we have chosen, and I remind myself of that over the weeks to follow. "Here we stay," I repeat to myself, laughing at the grimace I can hear even in my thoughts. We have recently returned from a week with my parents in Florida, and our bodies, if not our resolution, have softened in the subtropical air.

This was our first long holiday since buying the farm three years ago, and we had prepared feverishly. Anil had cleaned pens and stockpiled feed while I wrote an exhaustive list of directions, laughing at my compulsive need to cover every contingency. Then, the night before we left, the pipes froze solid in the milk room. Despite Anil's best efforts, the water refused to rise, and there was nothing he could do.

I was stunned, almost confused in my worry. He had dealt with frozen pipes so many times; how could we leave our new farm sitters with no water? Anil was matter-of-fact, an unruffled counterpoint to my distress. They could fill buckets in the bathtub and carry them to the barn, he assured me; it was no big deal. I conceded that it could be done, but it was a huge inconvenience, more than we should ask. Still, seeing no alternative, I scribbled an apologetic P.S. on my otherwise organized instructions: "Pipes are frozen—sorry—carry water from the house."

Reluctantly rebooting the computer, I searched online for our favorite technicians. Their website was reassuring, reminding us that they were available twenty-four hours a day, for any type of emergency. Still, knowing the cost of emergency services, I sent my SOS via e-mail: "Help— away on holiday—no water in barn, farm sitters need help."

Hitting the SUBMIT REQUEST link, I watched as my message was replaced by blue skies and a short confirmation. I sat in the darkened office as if waiting for a personal reply, thankful for technology but wishing for the comfort of a human voice.

We spent our week in Florida, a few minutes' walk from the beach. It was an alternate universe, and Keiran was confused by the strange forms of nature. He clung to us anxiously when we left the house, crying at the palm fronds swaying above his head. Back in the condo, he looked through the sliding glass doors but stiffened his legs when I tried to lead him outside.

Desperate for reassurance, I phoned the repair company, begging them to attend to the barn before Christmas. I hung around the phone like a lovesick teen, checking the answering machine for messages. A few days later I received my relief via e-mail—the briefest of notes: "Problem fixed." There were no details or explanations, but in a way I was glad to be left in ignorance, not knowing the expense.

We returned home at night to a car that wouldn't start, its battery refusing to turn over after a week of cold. While Anil coaxed the battery, Keiran and I waited alone in the terminal, the rest of the passengers long since departed. Keiran's patience exhausted, he ran frenetically between the luggage belts and the plastic Christmas trees, trying to grab the lights that blinked with a cheer I no longer felt. The night stretched itself out, the terminal a gray plastic world we could not escape.

Finally, the door slid open to the warm face of my husband, and I heard the car's engine idling outside. It was a relief to emerge into the night and feel time moving again. The air did not seem as cold as I had feared, and the much-predicted ice storm had not materialized, taking the dread out of the long drive home.

As the car headed north, pushing its way through the blackness, the night seemed darker than I had remembered but a little warmer in its embrace, welcoming. It was a relief to be in our own car, small though it was, heading back to the farm. As we finally turned down our road, the car bumping over the frozen ruts, I felt a rush of delight to be coming home, in a way that I never had before.

If night revealed the depth of our commitment, morning cast its pale light on another reality—the cost of leaving. The animals were fine, but the farm sitters, afraid of further damage to the pipes, had never turned off either the propane or electric heaters.

Facing the true cost of our vacation, I was so scared that I felt sick. That week alone would cost us hundreds in energy bills, plus the as-yet-unknown bill for the plumbing. I vented a little to Anil, but mostly I was quiet, worried that we were attempting the impossible. Could we make it? Were we living in a fantasy world? Would we end up only with debt? As yet we had no real farm income, but the bills, as we slowly restored the farm, were only too real.

With the temperature predicted to plummet and only a little propane left in the tank, I focus my immediate concern on preventing further damage. I beg the propane company for a quick delivery, presenting our case as animal welfare. However, they already have a schedule of needy customers, and make no promises.

For the next few days, I hover by the windows, watching for their truck. I am afraid they won't deliver to the barn, as we had changed our fencing during the summer, blocking their previous access. I leave bright orange directions stapled to the fence, the paper flapping wildly in the bitter wind. By Friday afternoon they still haven't delivered, and, with single-digit temperatures forecast, we are left no choice. Reluctantly, we turn the heat on. All weekend we monitor the temperature, turning the heaters off whenever we can, praying the fuel will last.

Monday I see the propane truck passing our house. With no time to dress Keiran, I secure him in the living room, closing the gates. Grabbing only a hat and boots, I run out, flagging down the delivery man. Bemused by my flustered state, he follows me through gates and under wires to the empty tank, nodding in time with my nonstop chatter.

Bursting back into the house, to my child and the warmth of the stove, I let out a huge sigh of relief. I pick up Keiran and twirl him around until we both laugh. "No frozen pipes," I sing, "no frozen pipes," and for a moment I forget to worry about the cost.

When he arrives home, Anil is glad to hear my news. However, he declares, with a sigh of resignation, this is the *last* time he is leaving the farm until we have trained farm managers. Looking at his resolute face, I remember Shirley laughing about their honeymoon: "It is a good thing we went away, because we never did again . . ."

This is the land that we have chosen, the farm that we have bound ourselves to, like a marriage that bears all seasons, for warmer or for colder. We have no regrets; we have become farmers, and we love our life here. We have forgone family gatherings, missed out on weddings, bar and bat mitzvahs, and graduations. When I write our apologies, I wonder what others must think of our life, tied to the farm by lustful bucks and pregnant does.

But the same roots that keep us here have drawn others in, in the energetically whirling circles of family reunions and the focused solitude of individual visitors. It is a sacrifice to miss others' events, but it is the reality we have chosen. To compensate, we have painted spare rooms and bought inflatable mattresses, opening the doors of our farm, sharing our great gift.

And if fewer people visit in winter, we do not wonder why.

January 2010

Thaw!

J ANUARY HAS tallied one windstorm, two power outages, three snowstorms, and countless single-digit nights, but the calendar confirms that we have finally reached the last days of the month. Awoken at 4:30 a.m. by my small daughter's internal squirming, I snuggle against Anil, absorbing the soft relaxation of his body. He shifts, wraps his hand around mine, generous even in sleep.

I try to lose myself in the shapeless darkness, but my mind rolls with my daughter's exertions, reminding me of all I need to do before she arrives. Only nine weeks left, if we are lucky. The churning of my mind is dispelled by the immediate needs of my body, and I turn slowly, revolving around the anchor of my belly. With more effort than grace, I push myself to sitting, struggling to emerge from the heavy blankets.

Bracing myself for the shock of the cold wooden floor, I am surprised to find the boards strangely warm. As I descend the stairs to the first floor, I hear water dripping from the roof. Excitedly I pull the curtains and peer blindly into the night. Snow melting at this hour can mean only one thing—January thaw!

Like a longed-for guest, here too briefly, the January thaw is a fairly predictable but unexplained weather pattern of the Northeast. Although climatologists debate its reality, statistics support local knowledge: Chance alone can't account for the frequency with which the third week of January brings a 6- to 10-degree rise in temperature.[1]

Often following a period of intense cold, the thaw is a welcome reminder of spring, clearing fields of snow and roofs of ice. The brief warmth returns color and smell to the landscape, the earth suddenly redolent of moist soil, waiting for the spring. If we emerge but briefly from the long tunnel of winter, it is enough to sustain us, at least until the endless days of March.

Although the landscape moves with a new fluidity, the house is strangely quiet, and I realize that neither of our cats is occupying its normal spot on the couch. All winter they have spent their nights alternately sleeping and wrestling, leaving scattered puffs of fur like milkweed down on the floor. Turning on the light, I can see the rug is clean, and I realize they have been outside all night, irresistibly drawn into the warm night air.

When Keiran awakes, he looks around forlornly for his playmates, the cats' ball held limply in his hand like a broken toy, suddenly useless. "Meow?" he questions, and I show him the patches of bare ground that have emerged overnight. Surprised, he examines the small blob that remains of his snowman, its carrot nose sticking straight up.

Already it is in the 40s, and I, like the cats, am impatient to emerge from the house. It is a relief to dress Keiran in a light jacket and boots, without the struggle of snowsuit and mittens. Watching him trudging joyfully up the road, I realize that his balance and strength have increased enormously. The snow and ice had forced him to maintain a tentative pace, each step deliberate. Now, on clear ground, he moves with freedom, the dirt reassuringly predictable.

Confident of his destination, he heads directly for the barn, and I merely open the gate, standing aside to let him pass. The animals too seem excited by the warmth, the goats once again sleek and lively. The pigs gallop the length of their pen, barking in excitement, and, for the first time, Rhodora lets me scratch her back. Redman snorts in indignation at such attempted familiarity, but he snuffles my hand, his nose soft and wet on my bare skin.

Leaving the barn, I aim Keiran for Don and Shirley's house, but he is magnetically drawn to the open doors of Don's tractor shed. In the dim light, the tractors stand tall and silent, improbably large beasts in the low-roofed shed. Keiran approaches them with new confidence, reaching up to investigate their sides, his hand disappearing in the grooves of their tires.

"Up, up," he begs, so I hoist him to the seat, its battered cushion tied together with an old shirt.

With Keiran happily absorbed, I am free to look around the shed, its walls adorned with all the necessities of farming. Tools, new and old alike, are hung neatly, waiting for the hand to pick them up. They are the tools of generations, many so old I do not know their names, much less their purposes. What knowledge will we lose, I wonder, when they are taken down for the last time, destined for the antiques store or scrap heap? Would we know what to do if we had to rely on our hands for survival?

A small yoke, sized for calves, hangs by the window, while a full-size yoke commands the opposite wall, so much larger that it seems made for an entirely different animal. Noticeable among all the wood and iron, a brightly colored weed whacker leans in the corner, eyeing the nearby scythe with contempt. I laugh but am not surprised, for Don is a practical man. After a lifetime of hard work, he appreciates tools that save his time—and his back!

Only after Keiran has "driven" both tractors can I lure him back to the ground. I urge him up the Hewetts' driveway by pointing out the wagon and old truck that line the drive, but thrice he turns back, drawn by his own imperative.

"Don, Don," he pleads earnestly, pointing at the tractor shed.

Like the beloved moon, Don had recently entered Keiran's vocabulary as a person of great importance. In his world, the connection between Don and tractors is clear and important. When we read together, he points out tractors with great excitement. "Don, Don," he says, turning to watch my face, needing me to understand.

"Is that Uncle Don's tractor?" I ask, and, satisfied, he turns back to his story.

Balking at the distant formality of "Mr. and Mrs. Hewett," I have adopted the Hawaiian tradition of respectful familiarity, and to Keiran they are "Uncle Don" and "Aunt Shirley."

Don has become one of the great men in his life, a point of reference for how one should live. At mealtimes, considering his options, he would often ask me, "Dada?," wondering if Dada ate that food. After seeing my father at Christmas, he had started to inquire about "Gampa's" food preferences, as well. Now, bagel in hand, he pauses to ask, "Don?," eager to know if Don eats bagels, if Don drinks milk, if Don likes split peas.

Recognizing his interest, I show him a photo album on loan from Don and Shirley, turning pages filled with photos of Don in the barn, feeding and milking the cows. He watches, rapt, then peruses it himself, turning the pages over and over.

"Cow, cow," he repeats, adding this to Don's list of great achievements.

Soon I realize that he recognizes Don's blue pickup and watches for it out the window, each passage a marked event. The next day I find a blue Matchbox truck parked by his toy tractors.

Now, torn between the man and the machine, he hesitates on the road, his compass pulling him in two directions. Only the discovery of mud puddles, freshly formed in the thawing ground, brings him—literally—back to earth. Fascinated by the suddenly fluid ice, he steers from one puddle to the next, splashing with great intent, watching as the water sloshes against his boots.

By the time we navigate their long driveway, Shirley has spotted us and is waiting by the door, eager for her little visitor. He goes boldly in, stopping to admire the photos of Don on his tractor. They have amassed a collection of tractor photos, framed testaments to the years of work that Don has put into the farm. More than the changes, however, what strikes me are the similarities—in each one a young child sits on Don's lap, beaming atop the tractor.

My child, meanwhile, has disappeared into the living room, eager to get to his "work." A regular visitor, he knows where the toys are, and he soon has all of the farm equipment spread out. While he drives model tractors around the couch, I tell Don and Shirley how he had spotted the open door and taken a "drive" on the *other* tractors. Don nods, glad that his tractors had gotten some work. "I opened the door to let some air in," he tells me, as if the tractors, like the beasts in the barn, fretted in their confinement.

Shirley and Don always have stories, running seamlessly from the news of the day to the memories of the past, and time passes quickly. Only when I notice Keiran banging the toys in frustration do I realize that we need to go. Shirley draws him in for a kiss, and he submits without protest, but when I ask him to give Don a hug, he pauses, considering the man sitting before him. Finally he goes over to him, arms half open, in the first real attempt at a hug I have seen.

When we return home, we find the cats sleeping, stretched out in abandonment, all play forgotten. Exhausted from the night's adventuring, they do not notice the passing of their inquisitive friend.

As I tuck him into bed for his nap, I know we still have months of winter ahead, but today has been a gift, a messenger of things to come. Bringing in wood for the stove, I hear the tractors' engines rumbling and know Don is waking them up, reminding them of spring's approach.

NOTE

1. http://www.islandnet.com/~see/weather/almanac/arc2002/alm02jan2.htm.

February 2010

Change of Light

A LTHOUGH THE thaw quickly surrenders to single-digit nights once again, there is a change in the light that quickens my pulse, reminding me of the sky and the new life waiting in the earth—and in me. Still, a promise, however hopeful, is only that, and the reality of winter yet demands our attention.

We monitor the temperature outdoors like a cardiogram, the small efforts of our heaters the lifeline to the barn's water supply. Like impoverished physicians, we dole out the least medicine possible, keeping the room hovering above freezing. I run in and out, turning heaters on and off, praying for enough residual heat to make it to morning.

Thankfully, inside the house the woodstove reigns supreme, and we indulge ourselves with near-tropical temperatures. Like a radiant beast, safely secured in its own pen, the stove eats with a vigorous appetite, the wood popping and shifting in the heat of its maw. In the morning I clean out the refuse of its meals, the ash, like manure, destined for summer fields.

Our firewood—split and seasoned ash—was a gift from my father, the product of his German sensibilities. A mix of perfectionist and

artist, my father was neither the fastest nor the most practical woods-
man, but the wood was near perfect in its completion. Each summer
morning he spread freshly split wood to dry on the barn ramp, collecting it again at night. Only when it had sun cured a few days did
he stack it, topping each day's work with a dated shingle, its vintage
recorded like a fine wine.

If my father delighted in the artistry of the wood, Keiran was equally
captivated by the physicality of the endeavor. When I bring in our day's
supply, glad to release the bulging log carrier, he rushes to explore, testing
his strength against logs of various sizes. Persistent as a small ox, he hauls
them around the kitchen, stacking them in various piles. Finally satisfied
with his arrangement, he then "splits" it with his wooden hammer, releasing a rain of sawdust and bark.

Only after I have loaded kindling into the stove does he hand me the
wood, piece by reluctant piece.

"Big," he says, his face reddening as he struggles to pick up the largest
pieces, and then "'trong," proudly, as he more easily lifts the smaller logs.
We pause for a moment to watch the flames catch and spread, proud of
our success, before shutting the stove door.

With the stove now bellying out a satisfying warmth, we turn to the
other matters of the day. The fields outside might be frozen solid, but in
the warmth of the house, there is hay to mow. With careful and endless
precision, Keiran drives a small toy tractor up and down the contours of
the couch, pleased by the tread marks the tiny tires leave on the brushed
suede. At his request, I put on a CD of tractor songs and turn to the
breakfast dishes, humming, "The old green tractor's better than it used
to be . . ."[1]

When dishes—and field—have been attended to, I call Keiran into
the kitchen where I have spread a blue tarp, topped by potting soil, trow-
els, and empty flats.

"It is time," I announce, "to start our garden."

He looks out the window, surprised, as if expecting to suddenly
see green, but I shake a packet of seeds in invitation and he forgets his
doubts, running to look in the envelope.

Ever since seed catalogs started arriving in mid-December, I had divided their bounty, securing the new ones in my office, off limits to toddler hands, before handing him last year's collection. These went into his magazine pile, an eclectic assortment of alumni magazines, children's catalogs, and other harmless periodicals. Perusing them at his leisure, he could rip and crumple without reprimand, exploring the paper as much as the pictures.

One day he brought me a Seed Savers Exchange catalog, delighted to have found his favorite food—tomatoes! Intrigued by the orderly rows of color photos, he pointed to picture after picture: "'mato, 'mato, 'mato," amazed to find page after page of them. Occasionally he paused, carefully examining the green and orange varieties that were interspersed with the more familiar reds. Yes, I assured him, those too were tomatoes.

Pleased by this discovery, he climbed onto my lap, and together we perused the vegetables. Many he knew, recognizing his friends with interest: the garlic he had planted last fall, the potatoes he loved to scrub. Then it became a naming game: beans, beans, beans, beets and carrots and corn, lettuce, lettuce, lettuce, melons (yum!) and onions and peas.

The next day, the catalog was his book of choice again, and I was surprised to see how many of the unfamiliar vegetables he remembered. Seeing his interest, I gave him the Seeds of Change catalog. Like a promising sequel, this one expanded the plot, including full-page color photos of farmers. Young and old, female and male, families and individuals, they were all here, and he turned back and forth, studying the different gardeners, these smiling people surrounded by vegetables. Wait, I told him, just wait until the spring, and we will plant some of these in *our* garden.

Now, as Keiran had confirmed with a glance, it was not yet spring, but we could not wait if we hoped for onions this fall. The planting of onion seeds was one of my favorite acts of gardening, although, with winter still in control, it often seemed a foolhardy gesture of defiance. But the very boldness of hope—and with experience, the confidence of it—made it an act of affirmation, not hubris. In reality, it was driven not by optimism but by necessity, for the shortness of the Maine growing season did not allow us to wait until spring.

With Keiran beside me, it is more fun than ever to bend over the potting tray, mixing water into the soil, feeling it moisten and swell under our hands, as if life has already answered our call. For Keiran it is a total delight, and he alternates between the uncensored joy of dirt on his hands and the fun of using a trowel.

The seeds themselves are unremarkable, small and dark, and they disappear as we drop them onto the moistened soil. Bending over the tray, I show him how to find them, their slight angularity distinguishable from the more-rounded organic matter. With a final sprinkle of soil on top, we tuck them in, resigned—more or less!—to waiting.

Settling the trays in a cool and dark but not cold corner, I wonder what the early settlers did. I supposed they must have cooked without onions, although that seems a colorless world to me. When Keiran was nursing, I had forsworn onions and garlic, hoping it would ease his severe reflux. For five months I ate with love and hunger but without taste, subsisting on the blandest of diets. In light of his health, it seemed a small sacrifice, but when the doctor declared it safe to eat onions again, I felt as if one of my senses had been restored.

For months afterward I craved onions in all their variation, but most of all in their raw and most sublime combination: sliced fresh in a tomato and onion sandwich. Although a strange-sounding sandwich, I could not resist the combination of flavors and textures, the sweet juicy tomato mixing with the crunchy pungency of the fresh onion.

Tomato and Onion Sandwich

Spread sliced bread with mayonnaise. Top with thick slices of onion and tomato, preferably heirloom tomatoes and fresh onions. Sprinkle with salt and grind fresh pepper over the top. Settle a second slice of bread over the top to help keep the highly unstable ingredients in place. Sink your teeth in and close your eyes.

Although it would be six months before we harvested an onion, it was encouraging to start our garden, and that evening Anil and I finally took an evening to plan. Every year we put off our planning, afraid that a realistic assessment would show the farm to be doomed.

After three years of trying, we had to face at least one reality: It was not enough to farm on weekends and evenings alone—not if we wanted to be more than hobby farmers our whole lives. One of us needed to be home, working on the farm, full time, if we were to keep up, much less make any progress.

We also, desperately, needed a tractor. Even with a few animals, it was hard to do all the work by hand. In the winter the manure built up faster than we could cart it out, and in the summer the pastures needed to be mowed as we rotated the goats through them. But, of course, there was no way we could afford a tractor on one income. In truth, we were constrained on all sides—no time to farm and no money to make up the difference.

Worse yet, it seemed as if we were slowly going backwards. We knew from experience that the demands of a newborn would make farming a distant priority this coming year. In the fall we had made the difficult decision not to breed the goats, as we would scarcely have time to milk, let alone make cheese, once the baby arrived. Surveying our weedy garden, we had also reminded ourselves *not* to be seduced by seed catalogs into an excess of planting.

Having reminded ourselves of all that we could *not* do in the near future, it helped to remember our long-term vision. For, much as we loved the lifestyle, we were not farming only for our personal fulfillment. Ultimately, we wanted to develop the farm into an educational center, with both local and international programs for a variety of ages.

Using Anil's connections in Trinidad, we planned to facilitate exchanges with students of agriculture, allowing them to experience sustainable farming methods appropriate to the small scale of island farms. With international students in residence, I also hoped to foster linkages with the local community, to increase understanding of global culture and agriculture.

Since being on *this* farm and seeing its rich influence on Keiran's life, we had snuck in a few more goals. Children benefited from directly experiencing their connection to the natural world, and our farm was a perfect small paradise for their explorations. Perhaps summer camps or day programs; the details were for the future, but in some way we had to include children.

And since dreams knew no bounds, I often imagined a living-history component of the farm. Standing in the lofty main hall of the barn, I could see it beautifully restored, with photos of those other generations of farmers and working examples of old tools, so children could actually try their hand at the crafts of the past.

With visions of such a vibrant and connected community, we realized that we could not give up—that the farm was too rich a resource to let slide into neglect. For the health of society *and* our farm, we needed to bring the two together, in ways both old and new.

Before we could host people, however, we needed to have a working farm!

Given the increasing demand for artisan cheeses, we had decided that a goat dairy would have the best chance for commercial success. In fact, we realized that a goat creamery made both personal and financial sense. Not only would it satisfy Anil's love of livestock and my love of crafting, but, as a value-added product, it would allow us to retain more of the profit. We would keep our other operations home-based: a kitchen garden small enough to tend by hand, and a smattering of livestock to supply the freezer, and provide interest to visitors.

Revitalized—how could we be depressed when there was so much to work toward?—we turned to our plan with hopeful hearts. Realistically, we would not be able to do much on the farm for a few years—not until the children were more independent and able to help, or at least not hinder as much. In the meantime, what could we do to prepare, given our limited income and even more constrained time?

We refocused on our medium-term goals, trying to make sure we at least stayed on track. Milk was half our goal, and cheese—for sale!—the other. To sell cheese, we needed to be licensed, which required preparation of separate areas for milking (the "milking parlor") and milk handling (the "cheese room"). Although dairy equipment was costly, this year we could at least evaluate the barn for structural soundness and clean and repair the milk room in accordance with the dairy inspector's requirements.

Set down on paper, our goals looked both logical and achievable. As the weight of uncertainty lifted, I felt hope trickling in, and dared to grin at Anil. Surely, with our skills and commitment combined, we could be part of the next generation of farmers.

NOTE

1. John Deere American Music, Steve Elkins, prod. "The Old Green Tractor's." *Crazy About Tractor Songs* (Green Hill, 2009, CD).

FEBRUARY 2010

EARLY ARRIVAL

THE TEMPERATURE rises to the high 30s, and Keiran and I are drawn outside like migrating birds. I laugh at myself, remembering how the same temperature had seemed an impenetrable barrier in the fall but now was sweet liberation.

Keiran is sturdy in his boots now, and, with the road clear of snow, he is free to run, pounding out his own rhythm. Pausing by the stone wall, he looks inquiringly at the barren trees.

"App, app?" he asks, remembering his fall pastime.

"First the snow has to melt," I tell him. "Then there will be flowers on the trees. Only when the flowers fall will we see the baby apples."

I hoist him over the residual snowbanks that line the road, separating us from the lawn. The thaw has cleared the ground, and I can see debris from winter's tempest scattered on the grass. I am tempted to rake it, but it seems too bold an act, an invitation to winter to prove her strength.

The south side of the house is sheltered, and, with the afternoon sun on our faces, it is warm enough to sit on the stone bench and watch the birds. A continual stream of chickadees bobs back and forth to the feeders, ignoring the bossy jays that lurk on the hawthorn, complaining about their industry. A lone nuthatch slides unobtrusively along the trunk, head down as if trying to avoid notice. Less concerned, a woodpecker also hangs upside down, swinging in time to his energetic jabs at the suet.

These are the birds, like us, that have chosen to stay through the winter, although I credit them with far more endurance than myself. We have watched them all winter, and we know their habits, but it is fun to be on their side of the window, as if we have finally stepped off the frame and into the picture. For now they have the feeders all to themselves, but I know that in warmer climes, the swallows and sparrows, blackbirds, bluebirds, and occasional oriole are already gathering, remembering summer in Maine.

Cast in the low, golden light, the land is beautiful in its stillness, its angles revealed. The fields lie exposed, the stone walls running in unusually clear lines across the flattened brown grass, as if they had been built overnight. Without their leaves, the trees too are freshly defined, stretching their fingers to the sky. The snow will cloak the land in curves again, and in spring the sudden pushing of green will distract from her nudity. But for now, for one brief moment, she has laid aside her garments and revealed her beautiful bones.

The goats also lie in strange repose in the fields, their usual busy inquisitiveness abandoned. They must come for the warmth or the light, for the sweet succulence of the grass has long since gone. It seems a strange mirage of spring, and Keiran and I sit for a long time, content just to be outside. When I finally bring him in, he settles easily into his crib, lulled by the fresh air.

Bending over the computer, I quickly scan my in-box, surprised to see so many messages on a weekday morning. An e-mail from my brother in Washington, D.C., solves the mystery; while we have been luxuriating in sunshine, the rest of the Northeast has been having a snow day. Unused to snowstorms, they send photos of cars buried in snow, of huge snowbanks and delighted children with their first snowmen. In New York Anil's sister-in-law is home from work, while in Boston my sister-in-law decides to cut short her hospital stay and do her post-op recovery at home.

Looking up from the monitor, I readjust my eyes to the bright sunshine, grateful but somewhat disoriented. Normally storms followed a predictable track, passing by each of my brothers—D.C., Rhode Island, Boston—on their way north, until they arrived on my doorstep like weary travelers, determined to stay a few days. This year, however, some strange buffer had eased the storms before they reached us, keeping it unseasonably mild since mid-February.

Bemused, I turn back to my next message, an expected e-mail from a local friend setting up a date to get together. Her P.S., however, gives me pause: "My daffodils are up!"

Daffodils? *Daffodils?*

Unable to resist, I run outside, bareheaded and barefooted, to check. I see them even before I cross the path, their fat green tips pushing their way through the compacted soil.

While I stare in wonder, my mind has already leaped ahead: If the daffodils are up, so must be the garlic, which we usually don't see until early April. I pause only to slip on some shoes—the ground *was* still cold—then head back out to the garden. Lifting up the mulch, I immediately see green, just the tiniest tips, but unmistakably there, dotting the length of the row in the orderly pattern of cultivated crops.

My head reels—garlic already! I am not worried about the plants; the weather is predicted to stay mild for the next week, and the mulch will protect them, even if the temperatures drop. More it is the pace of the thing—as if some inner imperative were pushing us to an early spring without the full pause of winter. Normally, there were months and months of slow motion when life breathed slowly, if at all. When spring came, it was always in a hurry, and we reveled in the adrenaline rush of exploding life. Yet March still stretched before us, a month notorious for its lingering cold and stubborn resistance to spring.

But the warmth, the bare ground, and now this pulsing green, overwhelm my senses with evidence, pushing experience aside. "I am here, I am here," they sing, quiet but undeniable. "Spring," I allow myself to whisper, hearing the doubt and hope and fear all mingled in my voice. *Spring*, my mind repeats, laughing and trembling, for I know what else spring brings this year, and I know that she too can arrive early.

I am not inexperienced with early springs or early babies. Keiran, my firstborn, had arrived a month before his due date, slipping into our lives with the delicacy of an atom bomb. Announcing his imminent arrival with the sudden rupture of my waters, he had been born with eyes wide open, immediately fastening onto my soul.

Joy and beauty, love and wonder. The miracle of a new life: "First we were two, then we were three, but nobody came in the door."[1] My boundaries blurred and shifted, reaching out to wrap around our son, joined by love. The air between us shimmered, tangled in our web.

Although his birth was a joy, his prematurity caught us ill prepared. His room was only half painted, and boxes and baby gear lay scattered around the house. Far worse, however, was his vulnerability. Just as his body rejected my milk, so too did his soul tremble at its emergence, overwhelmed by the world.

For ten months I hardly slept, holding him upright after every feeding, hoping the small advantage of gravity would gain him a few extra calories. I sat in the dark for hours, rocking him while he cried, overwrought from stimulation. There was no break and no giving up, for the life of the body and soul are delicate things, easily broken.

We had endured, and Keiran had made the passage to sturdy farm boy, but I was not eager for another early arrival.

That evening I call Beth, eager to share the news of the garlic. Her husband Ken answers the phone, and he cheers at my news. An ardent fan of warmer climes, he is hard-pressed to complain about the unseasonable warmth, but he knows it is strange.

"It would be great if it didn't mean it was the end of the world," Ken remarks wryly, and I have to agree, as the fear of global warming seems only too real on a day like this.

Still, he is in a good mood, and I feel relief flooding me. Only one kind of news could so lighten his mood: Beth's cancer finally seems to be in retreat. For months Beth had been fighting hard, enduring extensive rounds of chemotherapy. Though she had suffered terribly under the onslaught of such heavy medication, the cancer seemed untouched. When she could bear no more, she had agreed to try another, generally less effective combination of drugs. I had despaired to hear the statistics, but she had focused on living. Now, it seemed, the cancer was responding.

Perhaps it was only a moment, a mirage of hope, but for now, I would take it.

Closing my eyes in relief, I see again the green tips of the garlic, heralding the improbable spring. Life had called to the garlic, and it had answered, knowing neither fear nor hope. If a frost killed it, it would sink back to the ground, resigned to dirt once again.

But we . . . we trembled and hoped and fought for life, with all of its beauty and pain.

NOTE

1. Credit to an unknown poet, paraphrased to me by Beth Ann Eisen.

Keiran standing on the dirt road that connects our farm to Don and Shirley Hewett's.

Keiran at the wheel of Don Hewett's beloved John Deere Model B tractor.

Fances Kennedy standing by the barn, 1913.

Don and Shirley Hewett on their wedding day, 1951.

Edith Hewett, 1917.

William Hewett (left),
with son Lloyd
Hewett, 1917.

Here we stay—our farm in the depths of winter.

The January thaw melts the snow off the lower fields.

A change in the light signals spring's approach.

Jones
Brook,
beloved
to every
generation.

Lloyd Hewett plowing, 1916.

Jane Nutting, 1917, soon to become Jane Hewett.

Keiran, eager to do some gardening.

The joy of boots.

The newest farm girl, Sarita May.

Erskine Academy
yearbook photo of
Shirley Brown, 1949.

Don Hewett with niece Jean Hewett, 1952.

Anil on the new Kubota, tending to the fields.

Don Hewett with his dairy cows, Christmas 1984. Photo courtesy of Stanford Brown.

Don Hewett on his John Deere, July 2002. Photo courtesy of John Armentrout.

Keiran and
the holy-moly
potato.

Beth Eisen and Smoky Payson. Photograph copyright Audra Medunitza.

Twilight on the farm as a full moon rises over the back fields.

PART III

SPRING:
WEAVING THE CLOTH

1916

LLOYD AND JANE HEWETT

THE ROAD is noisy with laughter as a wagon rumbles by filled with family, all eagerly talking. They are too happy to hurry, as their hero has already arrived: a young man in uniform, Lloyd Hewett, twenty-three years old, honorably discharged from service in World War I.

For almost a year, Lloyd had been stationed in Brunswick with the First Maine Heavy Artillery, but instead of being called up, he was now on his way home. Although he doesn't know why he was discharged—or at least he doesn't say—he suspects medical unfitness, his tall frame too thin or his feet too flat. He is disappointed, but he finds consolation in the cheerful company of his father William, mother Edith, brother Will, sister Alice—and, most intriguingly—Alice's good friend, Jane Louise Nutting.

There is only one empty seat in the wagon; his grandfather Francis had passed away in February at the age of seventy-three. Francis's death was a blow to Lloyd, as they had been especially close, sharing a love of farming. However unprofitable it seemed to the rest of the world, Lloyd knew the reward of farming was the joy of the work. Grandpa had worked long and hard, and now, finally, was at rest, but he, Lloyd, was ready to take up the reins—literally. Last year he had bought the farm adjacent to his parents' house, with plans to establish a dairy like his father's.

The energy of youth would serve Lloyd well in the years ahead, for the land hadn't been farmed in a while, and there were fields to plow and hay to bring in. The small house was sturdy but simple, its rough board walls still a testament to pioneer days. It was acceptable for him, a bachelor; but to attract a young woman and raise a family, it would need expansion— and paint! It had a large barn, but it too needed upkeep, and a milk room would have to be built. The only redeeming feature was the long shed connecting the house and barn, sheltering him from winter's full blast. The barn and house were, in fact, largely inseparable, for there was always work to do—threshing, fixing equipment, and tending to the stock: the dairy cows, horse, pigs, and, of course, the oxen, still the backbone of his farm.

Although farmers on better land had switched to horses, many Somerville farmers still kept oxen to work the rocky hills and boggy lowlands. With his land still in sod, Lloyd knew he would be better served by the sturdy plod of oxen. Following his father's practice, he planned to plow and reseed the hayfields every year, and grass roots resisted the plow, yielding only to a beast more stubborn than them.

Luckily his father often sent his brother to help, and young Will would lead the oxen while Lloyd guided the plow. Slowly but steadily they worked their way across the fields, the newly turned earth black in their wake. During haying season the oxen waited patiently while they pitched the loose hay into the wagon, more tolerant of heat and flies than horses. In winter the oxen were slow but steady on the ice, hauling sleds piled high with wood to fill the ever-shrinking woodpile.

For all the work he had to do, Lloyd didn't complain when Alice asked him to pick her up in Augusta, for then he might get a chance to see Jane. Since Alice had started teaching in Manchester, she had been boarding with Jane's family in Augusta, and the two women had become fast friends. Jane—Jennie, as she was affectionately known—was a warmhearted, easygoing young woman, and Lloyd was soon as eager for her company as his sister was.

In Augusta Jane worked as a bookkeeper in a clothing store, but when she visited Alice, she participated with zest in the activities of farm life. When she and Alice went gathering herbs in the woods, Lloyd found excuses to meet them for lunch, picnicking on the huge boulders that rested on his fields like sleeping whales. Even Edith couldn't resist Jane's cheerful practicality, watching with surprised approval as she donned an apron to help put up the corn. Many an evening, Lloyd found himself at his parents' table, looking across at her as she laughed with Alice.

Working alone on the farm, he found himself looking forward to Jennie's visits, and soon he found he could not wait for her arrival. When restless energy propelled him out the door, he rode his bicycle the twenty miles to Augusta. Other days he rode his horse to Chelsea, boarding it in a livery stable and taking the electric car to the city.

Time flew by while farm and relationship grew, and on August 1, 1918, Lloyd and Jane were joined in a simple marriage service at the parsonage of the Penny Memorial Church in Augusta. At twenty-one and twenty-four years of age, Jane and Lloyd committed themselves to building their own family farm, taking their place as the fifth generation.

These were optimistic times, and, despite the uncertainties of war, the economy was thriving, and prospects for a young family seemed good. On June 18, 1919, ten months after his parents' wedding, Lloyd Jr. was born. Jane, now mother as well as farm wife, juggled her new duties with her typical commitment and grace.

The war had diverted a lot of food to troops and allies overseas, so home gardens and canning had to fill the gap.[1] Luckily, Jane had joined a large and supportive family, and she benefited from shared experience. As Edith recorded in her recipe book that autumn:

Piccalilli—The Best Ever

I have used this recipe since 1915. Have just finished some on October 3, 1919. Jennie will do some tomorrow.

1 peck (¼ bushel or 8 quarts) green tomatoes, sliced, 6 onions sliced. Throw a cup of salt over this and let set overnight. In the morning, drain, add 1 quart vinegar, 2 quarts water, boil 15 or 20 minutes, then put in a sieve to drain.

Take 2 quarts of vinegar, 2 pounds brown sugar, 1 teaspoon allspice, ground, 1 of cloves, 1 of cinnamon, 1 of ginger, ground, and ½ teaspoon of cayenne. Put in a kettle and boil for 15 minutes, slowly.

Nor was family help confined to the practical; there was more than enough love to go around. Edith had cared for babies since she herself was a child, and she assumed the role of grandmother with her characteristic dedication. Indeed, the question was whether one baby would be enough to go around, and for three years Lloyd Jr. was the undisputed prince of the family.

Then, on June 16, 1922, Donald Hewett entered the world after an easy labor, pleasing not only his parents but the attending Dr. Odiorne, who was not known to tolerate nonsense from any patient, ailing or newborn. William and Edith, marking their anniversary on that day, added another grandson to their reasons for celebration. And if Lloyd Jr. felt less pleased at the arrival of a competitor, he found solace in his grandmother Edith's kitchen, where her stone crocks were kept full of cookies.

Molasses Cookies for the Boys

One cup of molasses, 1 cup of sugar, 1 teaspoonful of soda in ½ cup hot water, salt, cassia or ginger, one large half-cup lard or lard and butter, or lard and beef drippings. Do not mix too stiff (with flour). Would be good if only ½ cup of sugar was used. Milk may be used in place of hot water.

With everyone working together, the farm grew as quickly as the family. Luckily, William and Lloyd had chosen a profitable venture, for many other Maine farms were abandoned in the aftermath of the war, declining from 60,000 in 1910 to 39,000 in 1930.[2] Maine farmers could not compete with Western producers of beef, grain, or sheep.[3] At the same time, the demand for hay, one of Maine's best crops, was in decline as gasoline engines replaced horses on city streets and in farm fields. Automobiles also required better roads, which meant higher taxes, often a death knell for a land-rich but cash-poor farmer.[4]

In contrast, dairy farms were expanding their herds, improving both their animals and their management, leading to an increase in milk production per cow.[5] Best of all, given the difficulty of refrigerated transportation, it seemed likely that milk products would remain protected from Western competition. Indeed, though they did not know it, milk would soon replace cream as the product of choice, greatly increasing its marketable volume.[6]

While other farms were closing, Lloyd and William joined the ranks of successful dairy farmers. To accommodate a growing herd, William expanded his barn, making space for twenty-five milking cows, while Lloyd installed a cream separator. When cream was the product of choice, they had focused on high-butterfat breeds like Guernseys and Jerseys, but as the demand for milk grew, they gradually shifted to the higher-volume Holsteins.

The cream, destined for the thriving Turner Center Creamery, could now be delivered to a railway station in Cooper's Mills, only six miles away. The Wiscasset, Waterville, and Farmington (WW&F) Railway, a tiny narrow-gauge railway more optimistic than practical, delivered the cream to Wiscasset, from where it was transported to Auburn.

Like most successful Maine farmers, William and Lloyd had expanded and specialized to meet the demands of the commercial market. However, they had not forgotten the self-sufficiency of their forebears, and they always planted a large home garden. Between potatoes and turnips, squash and apples, the garden provided a big part of their living. They even raised their own beans for baking, not a small contribution on a Yankee farm! Carefully stored in the cool cellar, the garden's produce resurfaced in wintertime meals, its rich starchiness a welcome reminder of sun and green.

In addition to vegetables, they grew their own meat, raising beef cattle, pigs, and chickens. Slaughtered after the first frost of fall, the meat froze solid until spring, yielding its meat reluctantly to forceful cleavers. If an unexpected thaw softened the meat, Jane sprang into action, canning it before it could spoil. Home production was a lot of work, but its yield was fresh and delicious—and it would serve them well in the lean years ahead.

As if to herald their changing fortunes, Sebra Crooker's original homestead—now the property of the Bartlett family—caught fire in June 1925, while the men were away at a town meeting. Young Lina Bartlett, alone at home with her bedridden grandmother, Delia, called Jane, and together they carried Delia out of the house on an old horsehair couch.[7]

For Jane, such feats of heroism were to be short-lived, for a growing pain in her left leg was soon diagnosed as polio. Frustrated by her sudden handicap, she struggled determinedly to live a normal life. In 1925 they had traded a horse for their first car, an open-sided 1922 Dodge, of which Jane was the proud driver. When paralysis made it impossible for her to drive, Lloyd fitted a wooden block onto the clutch, allowing her to regain some independence.

As the decade drew to a close, William had a heart attack, forcing him to give up his active involvement in his dairy. Unwilling to abandon the farm, he hired Lloyd to run the barn. With two farms to oversee, Lloyd's time was in short supply, and his two young sons began to assume family responsibilities. Don began milking at the age of seven, competing with his brother Lloyd Jr. to see who could milk the fastest. Lloyd Jr., a man by comparison, learned to drive at ten years old, proudly guiding the car down the road to pick up the mail.

Despite their best efforts, the Hewetts' ill fortune seemed to expand and strengthen, pulling the nation in with it. Although Maine newspapers scoffed at the stock market crash of October 1929 as a Halloween bogeyman,[8] the years ahead would reveal the depth and breadth of its impact. Lasting more than a decade, the Great Depression wreaked havoc on the modern financial system, forcing people to turn to older systems of support: home production and community networks.

For the people of Somerville, being "backward" was suddenly an advantage. The skills of those earlier generations had not been forgotten and would carry their descendants through the hard times ahead. Life on a small farm, even a marginal one, still allowed families to put food on the table. For the first time in decades, the number of Maine farms held steady,[9] and, in Somerville, actually increased.[10]

Forced out of work in the mills, a small enclave of French Canadians moved to Somerville, looking for land. Although the newcomers were culturally and politically different from the older families, differences paled before the shared experience of adversity. In October of 1933, "the most heated political debate in town involved a bet over who would win the presidency, Roosevelt or Landon, with the loser being forced to push the winner in a wheelbarrow from the Hewett Road to the Jefferson town line,"[11] 1.7 miles away.

For Lloyd and Jane, the most important event of 1933 was not President Roosevelt's New Deal but the closing of the WW&F railway, effectively ending their market for cream. Although Roosevelt's Agricultural
Adjustment Act (AAA) aimed to boost farm prices by subsidizing farmers to reduce production of specific crops, no Maine crop was on the list
of eligible commodities, and thus, no Maine farmer benefited.[12]

Ineligible for the government's support, Lloyd and Jane, like much
of Somerville, survived on the goodwill of local shopkeepers. Lloyd relied
heavily on Bowman's Store in West Washington for credit in gas, grain, and
other farm inputs. When Jane sent the boys to pick up groceries, the owner,
Charlie Bowman, unable to read and write, told them to "have Jane set it
down." This she did, faithfully, tallying it against the value of farm produce
that Lloyd traded in. Years later, when she returned $600 to Charlie, he was
greatly surprised, having supposed it was only a few hundred.

These were years of financial poverty for Jane and Lloyd, years they—
and Don—would never forget. When Jane could not find two cents for
postage, she saved where she could. On her visits to family in Augusta,
she brought vegetables to sell to neighbors. Word got around, and she
expanded her route, soon selling eggs and chicken meat as well. She
became a correspondent for the *Kennebec Journal*, writing a weekly col-
umn on the town happenings. Although she was initially not paid, she
was given a free subscription to the newspaper, otherwise an unattainable
luxury. Much later, she would be paid by the inch, but the reward was
never as sweet.

The family had always pulled together, but now everyone's efforts,
however small, made a vital contribution. William, unable to handle the
heavy work in the barn, took his hoe into the garden where he carefully
tended the crops, nurturing both plants and family.

When the garden work was done, he would entertain his grandchil-
dren with stories about the farm.

"You're probably tired of the same old stories," he would begin,
hoisting Don onto his lap, while Lloyd leaned against his leg. Don, too
young to know his grandfather's reputation as a storyteller, reassured him,
"That's okay; you tell them a little differently every time . . ."

Jane, in turn, took to helping Edith with her weekly washing. One
on each side, they would hoist the heavy copper boiler onto the stove,

filling it with water and clothes. Together, the burden was lighter, and they found reason to celebrate. Gathered in William and Edith's dining room, the family shared many meals, making of them a thanksgiving.

However, Yankee independence and community spirit were not enough to endure a decade of poverty. The citizens of Somerville were proud of their tiny town, but the price of self-governance was high. With only three hundred residents, the tax base was too small to support the town's vital needs, given the high rate of poverty. In 1938 Somerville deorganized, turning over its governance in return for financial assistance from the State. After eighty years as a town, Somerville was once again an unorganized territory, officially a plantation of the State of Maine.[13] The future of Somerville, for so long proudly self-determined, now rested in the hands of an ailing state and nation. For farmers, only recently tied to market whims, their prospects seemed less secure than they had during their self-sufficient pioneer past.

NOTES

1. Russell, *A Long, Deep Furrow*, p. 313.

2. Day, *Farming in Maine*, p. 178.

3. Ibid., p. 170.

4. Ibid., p. 179.

5. Ibid., p. 63.

6. Ibid., p. 179.

7. Allard, French, Cranmer, and Milakovsky, *Then & Now: Patricktown/ Somerville. Volume Two: History*, p. 96.

8. Judd, Churchill, and Eastman, *The Pine Tree State from Prehistory to the Present*, p. 512.

9. Day, *Farming in Maine*, p. 179.

10. Allard, French, Cranmer, and Milakovsky, *Then & Now: Patricktown/ Somerville. Volume Two: History*, p. 12.

11. Ibid.

12. Judd, Churchill, and Eastman, *The Pine Tree State from Prehistory to the Present*, p. 518.

13. Allard, French, Cranmer, and Milakovsky, *Then & Now: Patricktown/ Somerville. Volume Two: History*, p. 12.

MARCH 2010

BIRTH

MARCH FIRST—one day into the longest month. Outside winter and spring vie for position, while inside my pregnancy reaches maturity. Keiran, accustomed to our daily routine, darts around me as I vacuum, delighted by the humming machine. This morning, however, my lower back aches and the tops of my thighs burn, radiating with a throbbing heat. Sinking onto the couch in great relief, I am overwhelmed by a wave of fatigue. I prop my legs on the coffee table, then stretch them sideways on the couch, but I cannot ease their aching.

Unable to cope alone, I call Anil home from work. While he entertains Keiran, I sleep and sleep, waking only to change positions, hoping to ease the pain in my abdomen. In the late afternoon I wake to a quiet house. Although I had scarcely noticed, it is a beautiful day, and I assume that Anil has taken Keiran out to do chores. Lulled by the sun, I drowse, waiting for their voices to rouse me.

Keiran comes inside in a rush of boots and excitement, calling for "Mama" and "bagel." I stagger out like a broadsided boat, and he clings to my side, his small hand holding onto my pants with determination. He is tired and hungry, and I am quickly absorbed in his needs, glad to give Anil a break. Only after he is settled in his high chair, happily piling his food into several heaps, do I look up to see Anil smiling at me.

"I saw Don," he says, and I grin, knowing there will be a story to follow. "He was singing," he says, "sitting under a tree and singing." He pauses, remembering, then adds, "Singing loudly."

I have never heard Don sing, but it is easy to imagine him under the tree, soaking up the sun, his song echoing the delight of the day. There is an unstudied joy—a grace—about Don that reflects the beauty of the natural world. His song seems a blessing, as if he were one of the spirits of the farm, welcoming spring. All will be well, I think, as long as Don is here to watch over the farm.

My reverie is interrupted, however, by Anil saying, "Oh, yes, I almost forgot—there is a nice big doe kid in the barn."

As so often happens with Anil's casual proclamations, I am caught unprepared. Given our decision not to breed the goats last fall, there is only one goat it could be: Jasara, a young Saanen doe. In the throes of her first heat, she had slipped under the fence and into the buck pasture. We had arrived home to find her accepting the amorous advances of our Nubian buck. Laughingly, we had referred to her as our teenage pregnancy, all the while hoping she had not, in fact, conceived.

It was, as Victorian England would say, an undesirable match. Although it was possible to breed a doe at six months, we preferred to wait until they were at least a year old, allowing them to gain full maturity without the strain of pregnancy. A dairy doe was a long-term investment, and she needed to tolerate the strain of repeated pregnancies and heavy lactation. In addition, we had decided to maintain purebred animals, and this was a crossbreed match. While crossbreeding could produce winners, it would also certainly produce losers. More importantly, there was the matter of the kids, and what to do with the yearly surplus of young animals. While buck kids were valuable for meat, doe kids could be sold as breeding stock—and a purebred animal fetched a higher price.

However, our wishes had not entered into this equation, and one plus one was now, in fact, equal to three. As I sit back, feeling the inevitable rush of excitement that new life brings, another realization startles me: Like the spring and the bursting garlic, the kid had arrived early! If we had expected a kid at all, it was in April, inconveniently the same month I was due. For a moment I am overwhelmed, as if all of nature is conspiring against patience. The baby moves inside me, her cramped wiggling somewhat painful, and I place my hand over her, pleading for a little more time.

For now, however, she is safely ensconced in her watery world, and, with Anil to watch Keiran, I am free to go outside and meet the new arrival. Although we usually separated new families, Anil has left these goats together, as Jasmine, the proud grandmother, was guarding mother and newborn. I am surprised, unfamiliar with such three-generational loyalty, but, peering into the pen, I can see they are well protected. Standing between the herd and the new family, Jasmine makes an impassable fortress, blocking an entire hayrack. While the rest of the goats cluster awkwardly at the other feeder, Jasmine remains vigilant, snorting her challenge.

Through her legs, the new kid is visible, already intent on finding milk. With unerring instinct, she aims for the underbelly, her head ducked to catch her mother's nipple. In contrast to Jasmine's vigilance, Jasara seems barely to notice her new kid. First-time mothers sometimes need help with bonding, bleating quizzically at the small new blob of goat, shifting away from its seeking mouth, their swollen udder too tender to touch. However, in a comical stereotype of a teenage mom, Jasara seems neither perturbed by the kid's advances nor concerned for its well-being.

This calm acceptance was one of the desirable traits of Saanens. As another farmer had remarked, Saanens were essentially milk machines, unmindful of assaults on their udders, be it goat, human, or machine. Indeed, we had been surprised last year to see the Saanen kids nursing from all the Saanen does, regardless of parentage. In marked contrast, our temperamental Nubian had been quite outraged at their advances, chasing the accosting kids away.

Although I have intended only a short visit, I linger by the fence, fascinated by the herd's dynamics. I am intrigued by this evidence of extended family ties, totally different from what I had witnessed as a child with our sheep. Once sheep weaned their young, they apparently forgot their relationship entirely. If they retained any notion of family, it certainly did not count against the greater enticements of feed, for which they competed fiercely.

In marked contrast, our goats remembered their offspring despite extended separation. We weaned the kids at six weeks, and all summer the kids ran in a separate pasture, calmly independent. However, when the herd was reunited in the fall, the families immediately regrouped, sleeping and eating together. There even seemed to be breed identification, as the herd naturally separated itself, the multicolored Nubians on one side, the solid-white Saanens on the other. Anil and I had laughed at such segregation, calling it racial discrimination, but the goats seemed contented in their divisions.

This multigenerational allegiance, however, is new to me, and I wonder how far it would have extended. In the future we intended to separate the kids at birth, as most farmers did, in order to facilitate our handling of them. Although it had been easy to leave the families together, the kids had grown up wild, flying on swift feet away from our advances—not an asset in a milking animal! In contrast, our senior does had been bottle-fed and instinctively moved toward us, accepting our handling with minimal protest.

For now, however, the family is intact, and Jasmine bleats in soft grandmother-speak to the kid, licking its head and hindquarters. She is an appealing little thing, an unlikely combination of long legs and delicate face that makes the most of her vulnerability. Although I had assumed the Nubian-Saanen cross would result in a colored coat, she is pure white, with no trace of her father's extravagance of color. Only her floppy ears proclaim her Nubian inheritance, adding to her somewhat comical appeal. I am tempted to name her, but I know she is destined for slaughter and would be better served by one of Anil's irreverent nicknames.

As she settles into the hay, belly full, I realize that I have come to peace with slaughtering the goats. Have I become hardened, I wonder, taking the goats' lives for granted? I do not believe so. I still feel the joy of their personalities and a pang of sorrow at their death. But this is reality: Life consumes life, be it animal or vegetable, and we cannot step off that wheel without ending our own.

In school, studying the intricate beauty of plants, I had become more aware of the *life* that coursed through them. We ate plants blithely, without remorse, but was their life any different from that of animals? Plants are, undeniably, closer to the dirt, their transition to the soil only a matter of days or weeks. But are they any less a part of life? We share energy, we share matter; life continually cycles through us all, changing form.

Most novice gardeners feel a pang of remorse when they first thin seedlings, watching their delicate bodies collapse. I too still marvel at the perfection of their miniature forms, but I do not feel a loss; they will soon be part of the earth again, the soil which itself teems with life, cycling, recycling. Knowing the science of life has immeasurably deepened the mystery of it, the wonder of life's endless transformations.

No, I don't think I've become hardened; rather, I'm constantly aware of and grateful for all that sustains me. This small kid, like my sprouting onions, will become part of my life, and is all the more precious for it. Feeling my own web of connections, I pull myself away from the pen and back to the house, my family waiting for me.

MARCH 2010

SPRING

ID-MARCH, just a few days shy of spring. Normally we observe spring's official entry with a wry laugh, as winter continues to blast us with seemingly endless ferocity. This year, however, spring is the uncontested winner, to everyone's disbelief. Don remarks that he has never seen a spring like this, and I feel the length and depth of his years, watching eighty-seven springs wash over these fields.

The rushing green transforms the landscape, swallowing last year's bent brown stalks. Migrating birds start to appear, vying for space at the suddenly full feeders. The red-winged blackbirds arrive en masse one morning, darkening the grass under the hawthorn as they search for spilled seed, the bright flash of their wing bars still more yellow than red. Robins arrive—two weeks early!—hopping hopefully across the lawn, heads cocked, listening for worms.

While I have struggled with the growing pressure of life inside me, wondering and waiting, spring has shown no such uncertainty in her arrival. Trying to prepare the house for the baby, I step outside to rinse our compost bucket and am instantly lost, seduced by the fresh delight of the air. Immediately—and without regret—I abandon all my plans. The baby may be coming, but spring is already here and must be celebrated! I call Anil and Keiran to join me, and we assemble in the garden, blinking and stretching, laughing at the pure delight of the day.

The overgrown garden is a forlorn testament to the neglect of the year before. Determined to keep the sun from awakening more weeds, we cover the dirt with tarps and cardboard. With my belly straining taut before me, I cannot tackle the larger clumps of grass, but I stick a tentative pitchfork into the looser soil around the trellis. Squatting carefully, I pull out the weeds, coaxing forth their long roots. Keiran shadows me, excited by this foray into the dirt. He stares in amazement at the unexpected emergence of the thickly branching roots, as startling as a subterranean Medusa.

Seeing his interest, I fetch a child-size rake and shovel for him, explaining how we need to make room for the vegetables to grow. "No weeds, no," I tell the uprooted plants, shaking my head in disapproval, "please don't grow in our garden." He is soon busy poking at the soil, the tools now comfortable in his hands, shaking his head and exclaiming, "No weeds." Together we move up the row, slowly but deliberately, delighted in our trail of bare soil.

Eventually remembering the other life I am tending, I straighten, hands on back and belly. I call Keiran, knowing we are late for lunch, but he is blind to all but weeds. When coaxing and cajoling fail, I carry him inside, forcibly separating him from his shovel. He eats and drinks through his sobs, then abandons himself completely to tears when I lay him in his crib. He cries in short, high bursts, lost to grief, until finally I gather him in my arms and rock him to sleep, his head and hair damp with tears.

After I settle him back in his crib, I rush to check on the onions and leeks. In the cool temperatures of our bedroom, they have emerged so slowly that my daily misting has become an act of faith, the water darkening only bare soil. Today, however, I see their pale heads poking forth like sightless worms testing the air.

To prepare for life outdoors, they will need light, so I carry in the seedling box, a light wooden frame enclosed by plastic, holding the all-important grow lights. Morning and evening I will impersonate the sun, brightening and dimming their world with the bulbs' pale luminescence. In a few days the seedlings will flush green with chlorophyll, stretching eagerly toward the lights. Like hundreds of tiny green bows, they bend as they grow, their tops held fast beneath the soil while their stems rise taller and taller. Eventually released, they spring up, carrying their tiny seed aloft like a small flag of triumph.

As I settle the last of the seedling trays in their new home, I hear Keiran calling, "Mama, Mama, Mama." Relieved to have finished before he woke, I greet him with a cheerful smile. He, however, has not been distracted by sleep, immediately demanding, "Rake, rake."

Amused at such attachment, I wash off his tools, and he carries them around proudly, raking and digging wherever he is allowed.

Seeing his sustained interest in the garden, I waver, wondering if I should share the excitement of the new onions. I had not planned to introduce them yet, expecting his curiosity to outweigh his restraint. Eager as we are to engage him in gardening, we were hoping to first introduce him to larger seeds in the sun-warmed soil of the garden. But with temptation so close, I cannot resist, and I open the door to the dining room and point.

Enclosed in clear plastic, the seedling box is a small planet of its own, a glowing world in the quiet dimness of the room. Propelled into orbit, Keiran runs to the box and lifts up one corner, looking at me in inquiry.

"Those are the onions," I tell him, "the baby onions we planted."

Intrigued, he reaches in to touch, so I caution, "Be gentle with the babies."

He struggles to obey, his curiosity warring with his desire to please, brushing his hand along their quivering tops.

Seeing that we are destined to spend some time with the seedlings, I decide we might as well water them. One tray at a time, we carry them into the comfort of the kitchen, where I mist them with a hand sprayer. Keiran is fascinated by the noise and action of the spray bottle and reaches for it, demanding a turn. All seriousness, he mimics my motions, sweeping the bottle over the trays, his face a study in joy.

When his curiosity is finally satisfied, I return the trays and close the door, shutting out the cold but not his interest.

"Baby, baby?" he asks me repeatedly, returning to the door, until I confirm that the baby onions are indeed growing in there, cold but happy.

Spying an onion on the counter, destined for that night's dinner, he demands, "Ony, ony," and holds out his hands. He turns its smooth sphere around and around, looking for a point of entry. The golden brown skin is taut and smooth, defying his efforts, so I show him a thin point at the neck where he can at least smell it. For a long time he holds it pressed against his nose, until I am afraid it will burn his eyes. When I ask for it, however, he holds it more tightly, so I turn to the pantry for a more-willing victim.

While I dice onions and vegetables for supper, I watch him playing in the living room, filling the air with his imaginary world. The onion accompanies him, for the moment a cherished companion. Occasionally put down but never abandoned, it is carefully retrieved after each adventure. Only as the light fades does his energy wane, his stories slowing. Surprised by his silence, I look up to see him lying on the floor, the onion snuggled next to him.

March 2010

River

AS THE month draws to a close, the rain falls day and night. Confined indoors, we sit by the window, waiting for the clouds to break. I feel trapped, my freedom confined by my swollen body. Beth has predicted my daughter's birth on the full moon, and I feel its approach like the pulling of tides.

I wake in the dark, hours before dawn, pulled from sleep by alternating hope and fear. My daughter shifts inside me, bracing her feet against my side, raising my abdomen in a rolling swell. It is an oddly uncomfortable feeling, and I rub my hands over my belly, hoping to quiet her. I am excited to meet her, eager but uncertain, unsure of the signs of a regular labor. We have already made several trips to the hospital, reassured by the nurses that my incessant cramping was not yet productive.

The hospital . . .

My thoughts shift, darken, for endings as well as beginnings hover over its sterile hallways. The brief hope of Beth's trial drug has succumbed to the implacable advance of the cancer, and she has retreated to the hospital, desperately seeking fortifications. In a horrible irony, the cancer has colonized her stomach, mocking her consummate skill as a chef. Food has turned to poison in her body and is violently rejected, weakening body and spirit. Unwilling to accept defeat, she has agreed to intravenous feedings, to life without flavor or texture, her spirit still bound to this world.

Unable to lie still under the weight of my thoughts, I head downstairs, wrapping myself in a blanket. I sit on the couch, opening a crack in the curtains, peering into the void. The fragility of life—the possibility of Beth's passing—stares bleakly back at me without compromise. We exist in this moment only, pausing between birth and death, until we too pass. Beth knew it, celebrated it, and struggled with it. Ever the artist, she had etched its imprint on homemade paper, the letters floating as improbably as an individual life upon the fabric of time.

There are only two stories
The stranger comes to town
Or
One goes on a journey
Actually there is only one story
The story of your birth
You are the stranger in town
You are on a journey

Now, at last, she faced it, the final journey—no escape, just painful delay.

The dark yields reluctantly to the impatient advances of the spring sun, the gray light warming to reveal a landscape defined by frost, each blade of grass whitened. The trees, still bare, appear lifeless except for the eager hopping of birds, white breasts flashing, feathers shaking. Freshly returned, the summer dwellers are in hot pursuit of food, shelter, and mates. Their busy voices penetrate the storm windows, their songs sweeter and more elaborate than the brief, harsh calls of winter's denizens. Like melting snow, their voices warble and trill, water running, released to flow. *Life, life returns*, they sing as they hop, comically hopeful as they bob across the yard. Defiantly deaf, the naked trees remain still, unmoved.

If the morning is too clear, the day is a blur, the endless rain blending into my endless fatigue. I head to bed early, unable to sustain an interest in the day. When Anil comes in, I roll over, then rise quickly in a rush of water. I feel a bubble swelling, bursting, a seemingly endless waterfall crashing on the floor. Suddenly there is no past and no future, only the present spilling onto the floor, and the need to act. Fatigue, indifference, fear—all dissolve into the clarity of the moment, swallowed by the ocean washing down my legs.

Swaddling myself awkwardly with towels, I grope my way past Kei-ran's door, heading for the phone. My parents will stay with him while we are away, so I have prepared a "fun bag" to distract him from our absence. He loves his grandma and grandpa, but this will be his first time without us, and I feel a pang at leaving him. Although it is a small separation, I know it is the first of many, and my hands tremble as I dial the phone, connecting my parents and my children.

My father's voice, foggy with sleep, is calmer than mine—I have already summoned him on several false alarms. He laughs when I tell him there is no turning back; it will be his birthday in a few hours, and he doesn't mind sharing! Relieved to finally be in action, I grab my hospital bag and a few extra towels for the road.

As we back out of the garage, rain splashes across our windshield, and I try to relax into the small world of our car. We have an hour's drive to the hospital, and the rain will not allow us to hurry. If the moon is guiding us, it is invisible behind the full belly of the clouds, and we proceed in watery darkness, relying on the blurry glow of our headlights. The windshield wipers do their rhythmic best, steadying me as I time my contractions.

They know us well in the maternity ward, and I am quickly settled in, the bright corners of the delivery room replacing the vague wash of the night. There is no need to confirm my labor this time, and I am soon given over to my task. Later Anil will tell me that it rained all night, but for now I know only the small world of my body. Vaguely I know we have passed into tomorrow, but it is not until the doctor enters, bleary-eyed, that I realize the hands of the clock have turned to morning.

The doctor's presence can mean only one thing: The baby is ready—and I am free to push! Wanting to witness her emergence, I look into the mirror curiously, orienting myself. Amidst my own stretched anatomy, a wrinkled black patch appears, and I pause, surprised by my furry off-spring. The doctor laughs; it is hair, she assures me, the normal top of a squished head. Then I need to push, and, with effort, I transform it into a small head and, once again, an improbably big head. Now there is no time to exclaim, for suddenly there are shoulders and a rushing slide of body, returning the head to its proper proportions.

Mother, father, doctor, nurse—we all laugh, our wonder unconfined by parentage, and I am rewarded with the small, wet body of my daughter on my chest. The chalky vernix that coats her skin smells sweet, and I am reminded of the goats that lick their newborns with such thorough atten-tiveness. Here it is the nurses who clean babies, removing the remnants of their former homes. Still, I am glad for these first raw moments, and the sticky glue that binds us together. Eyes closed, we breathe into each other, alone for one last moment. Then Anil bends over us and she opens her eyes, joining the world: Sarita, river girl, washed in with the rain of the full moon.

A few hours later, the medical welcomes are complete, and it is a decent hour for visitors. I hear Keiran before I see him, the high pitch of his endless questions and the deep rumbles of my father's replies. As they knock, I settle Sarita in her bassinet, prepared to welcome my firstborn with full attention. He comes in by himself, grown—in both our estima-tions—into a big boy. Resplendent in a new (to him), larger pair of bright yellow boots, he tromps around proudly, fascinated by the sound of his heels on the floor.

Having made the desired entrance, he turns to the next issue of importance: finding his sister. Apparently unconcerned by my short absence, he uses me merely as a step to lean over Sarita's bassinet. It is hard to convince him to look and not touch, and I restrain his grabbing hands as unobtrusively as possible. Unconcerned, she sleeps on, and he gradually loses interest, telling me instead about his boots.

Hand-me-downs from his cousins, the boots are several sizes too large and were supposed to still be in storage. However, he had spied them sticking out of the box and had begged my parents to wear them. Unable to part him from them peacefully, they had given in, deeming them suitably celebratory.

I grin at my parents, familiar with Keiran's obsessions, glad that he has something new to excite him. Still, when he realizes I am not coming home yet, he clings to me, outraged to be parted again. Advised by an experienced parent, I am prepared with a parting gift: "something," they had recommended, "totally irresistible." I hand him a gift bag and he rustles the paper aside, then pauses, delicately touching the small red tractor that nestles inside. When my father bends to pick him up, Keiran looks at me blindly, his world completely focused on his new toy, unaware of his own departure.

Anil follows them out, heading home for a quick check of the goats, and I am finally alone with Sarita. I bend over the bassinet, free to focus on the mystery that is my daughter. The need to hold her is overwhelming, and I brush her soft, dark hair, then hesitate, remembering the date: March 31. With the room quiet, I have time for one quick call before she needs to nurse; for today is not only my father's and Sarita's birthday, but also Shirley Hewett's.

1935

SHIRLEY BROWN

A CAR MOVES slowly down the road in the unmistakably ponderous pace of a funeral procession. Shirley Brown, four years old, sits in the back seat, longing for a hand to hold. She looks at her father in the front, wishing she were next to him, held close against his warm side. She doesn't understand why she has to sit next to her grandmother, so straight and stiff, her face as stern as her black dress. The car moves so slowly that Shirley fears they will never get to the cemetery, and she wiggles in the uncontrollable agony of restraint, wishing herself away.

She had been startled by the casket that stood tall and dark in the center of her mother's room and had looked around wonderingly for the missing bed. There were lots of people there, and someone spoke kindly to her, explaining that her mother wouldn't suffer anymore. Shirley knew that was a good thing, for her mother had been sick for a long time. The doctor had been a frequent visitor at their house, but his medicines were powerless to stop the advance of her mother's illness, and she had slowly weakened. Eventually she had stayed in bed, where Shirley would visit her, bringing some fresh delight of the farm to share.

There was so much to do and see on the farm, and Shirley wanted to be a part of it all, running to keep up with her father. Watching the two of them heading out to the barn, her mother would say with a smile, "There go my two farmers." Although her father did road maintenance for the state, his passion was farming. His large barn was full of registered Hereford cattle, the best of which he sold for breeding stock. Shirley loved to watch them, their large, white faces peering curiously back at her, their stocky, brown bodies clustered against the fence. She was not afraid of the animals—except the bulls—and would walk underneath the workhorses, until the day her cousin's leg was broken by a startled mare. Only when an animal was slaughtered would she run inside, burying her ears in her hands.

In the summer, the days were long, and the outdoors tempted with adventure. During haying season, she carried drinking water to the men in the field, waiting eagerly for a ride home on the soft bed of fragrant hay. At day's end, her shoes, missing once again, were found by the stone wall, next to a patch of wild blueberries.

Tagging along with the hired hand, she went to explore the small spring that supplied water for the house. While he filled buckets with water, she went frog hunting. Excited to catch one, she carried it carefully home, but halfway there she tired and slipped it in one of the full pails. The housekeeper was not at all pleased to discover the frog, and Shirley retreated, surprised; the frog had been in the spring, after all . . .

When the housekeeper's patience, worn thin by muddy feet and trails of hay, finally ran out, she locked Shirley out of the house. Alone, Shirley walked through the field, the freshly turned dirt like a rolling ocean around her. When her father spied her, he halted the horses, looking down at her serious face. After hearing her story, he pulled her onto his lap without comment, and together they harrowed the rest of the field.

Closer to home, her father's garden was a constant source of delight and temptation. The tall corn plants towered over her like a maze, inviting her in to wander. As she explored the rows, she would pause by the peas and cucumbers, admiring the tiny fruit, longing for their sweet freshness. Unable to resist, she would eat them standing in the garden, until her father found her, and, with gentle remonstrance, reminded her that there would be none for the table if she ate them all when they were small.

Trying to obey, she brought them to her mother to share their sweet delight. Slowly she fed them to her, her small fingers placing one after another in her mother's open mouth. Finally, however, her mother settled her head on the pillow, closing her eyes. "It's too hard," she said softly, and Shirley crept outside to find her father, leaving her mother to rest.

Now her mother would never get up again, and she could no longer follow at her father's heels. In debt from all the doctor's bills, her father could not afford to hire a housekeeper, nor could he stay home to care for her. She would go to live with her grandmother, some ten miles away. Her father would visit her on the weekends, he told her, smoothing her hair, and she looked back at him soberly, afraid to tell him her fears.

Two months later Shirley moved in with her grandmother, into the house where she would spend the balance of her childhood. Although she never told her father, she suffered terribly away from his tender warmth. Her grandmother provided for the needs of the body, but she did not understand a child's heart and soul. Shirley's vivacious spirit, once encouraged, was now met with disapproval and discipline. Curiosity, it seemed, was to be restrained, not expressed.

Over the years, Shirley often wondered why she could not win her grandmother's approval. Once she had known she was special. When her parents had told her that the doctor had brought her into the world, she had always imagined that he had arrived with two or three babies, and, from among them, her mother had chosen *her*. Now, it seemed, she was just a burden.

When her father came on his weekly visits, she'd sit on his lap, and the warmth of his arms would brush some of the loneliness away, but she knew he would soon leave, and a chill would descend again. To delay the separation, she'd follow him out to the car, keeping her eye on him as long as possible. Soon this comfort was to be denied as well, for her grandmother told her that at four years old, she was too old to sit on her father's lap.

With little affection to be had in the house, Shirley turned to the familiar delights of the barn. Her grandmother had a small farm, and every animal, from the pig to the workhorse, had a name. Shirley knew them all and was entertained by their personalities, their reliable quirkiness that did not scold or disapprove. The dairy cows were her particular friends: Betty, the fawn-brown Guernsey; spotted Sally, the Ayrshire; and, most beautiful of all, the black-and-white Holstein, Pam.

Shirley looked forward to winter, when it was her job to bring the cows to the well. One at a time, she would halter them and lead them across the road. Accustomed to their small shepherd, they would trot along eagerly, lowering their heads to drink as she pumped water into their trough. Only Sally, stubbornly placid, refused to be hurried, setting one slow foot in front of the other, much to the annoyance of her little courier.

When, inevitably, the cows went into labor, Shirley was frightened by the transformation in her gentle friends. Panting and scraping the floor, they seemed to struggle against an invisible enemy, and she would run into the house, away from their distress. However, she knew the reward that awaited and would creep out a few hours later, peeking around the stall to catch a glimpse of the new calves, fascinated by their clean, almost translucent hooves.

From the ages of five to thirteen, she attended the Corner School, a one-room schoolhouse ten minutes' walk away. Most of the teachers boarded with her grandmother, so she had little excuse for not learning her lessons. Not surprisingly, she did well in all subjects except math, her perpetual nemesis. Standing at the blackboard, she would freeze in anxiety when the teacher challenged her calculations. Next to her she could hear a classmate faintly tapping out the answer, but she dared not look, afraid of being rebuked for cheating.

Freedom—and happiness—finally came for Shirley in the fall of 1945, when she entered Erskine Academy, a co-ed school in the neighboring town of South China. To her relief, there were no buses during the week, so she boarded at the school. Although there were plenty of rules, the teachers were fair and friendly, and she flourished away from her grandmother's stern discipline.

Eager and bright, Shirley participated in everything from basketball and softball to plays and hiking. Vice president her freshman year, she was class president by her senior year. "Spitfire," her classmates called her, and in her senior photo, her eyes dance, her vivacity restored. She had done well, and her elder brother encouraged her ambition, urging her to go to business school in Boston. These were modern times, with new opportunities for educated young women.

Still, she hesitated, remembering the farm and the solace of animals, and in her yearbook, her stated ambition reflected an older, quieter longing: *Farmerette*.

April 2010

Family Farm

PRIL HAS arrived, and, driving home from the hospital, I realize that spring is no longer a promise but a reality. Lawns and fields are turning green, their color washed in with the life-giving rain. Still close to the edges of creation, we look out at the world with fresh eyes as if, like Sarita, we were driving these roads for the first time. In the backseat her small body looks lost in the car seat, the hugeness of her existence housed in her tiny form.

Turning onto our road, I feel the familiar rush of gladness as the wheels bump over the gravel, chanting *home, home* . . . As I enter our house of many generations, Sarita in my arms, new life rushes in with me, as eager as the cats that run from room to room, inspecting their domain. It is a beginning.

The outside world recedes as we circle around Sarita's tiny being, our reality defined by her immediate needs. Night and day run into each other, the boundaries of light and dark obscured by her hunger, her small cries pulling me awake to a world blurred by fatigue. Forging the bonds of a lifetime, we build our connections with the most basic of blocks, passing life from my body to hers. She is more animal than human, grunting and squirming in her bassinet, scarcely knowing where she stops and the world begins.

My own awareness, in the endless fatigue of nursing, subsides to its most basic level. There is a strange amnesia of time, as if these first few months were a secret known only to us. Each day exists only in the present, days of love and bonding that we will never remember, that pass into the memory of the house. It alone witnesses these moments of love and attachment, adding new chapters to its story, life rising and falling.

Lacking a sense of days, I reckon time by Anil's presence, dreading the day he returns to work. Sunday arrives too quickly, but, in compensation, the day is warm and clear. The sun is bright enough to penetrate my haze, and I suddenly remember spring and long to feel the air. I look at Keiran, his small body taut with constrained energy, and propose a family walk.

"Yellow boots," he cries immediately, and scampers to the door, bouncing happily while we dress Sarita for her first farm outing.

Shielding her as much from the sun as the breeze, we bundle her in blankets until only her small, pink cap is visible. Keiran, equipped with his own hoe, sets to work as soon as he clears the door, uprooting the gravel on the driveway.

"Come on, Keiran," Anil says, "let's walk to the back field."

Keiran looks up, disbelieving. "Back field?" he asks, his hoe still poised for action. Moose occasionally walk through the field on their way to the brook, and Keiran often watched for them, scrutinizing the hillside for unusual shapes. During the winter, the snow had kept us closer to home, but now the fields beckoned invitingly, their brown already speckled with green.

With the promise of such an expedition, Keiran abandons his labors and the four of us set out, Sarita in hand and Keiran at heel. Diego, in typical cat fashion, follows us with deliberate nonchalance. Stalking the edges of the path, only the tip of his tail twitches with intent. The light is bright but soft, bathing the landscape with the freshness of spring. The green of the pines seems deeper in the clear air, and the sharp outlines of the leafless deciduous trees are softened by buds.

Freed from the frozen monotone of winter, the brook shines a brilliant blue, beckoning us to its side. We pause at its edge, held motionless by its rushing flow. Swollen with melting snow, it moves with swift energy across the stone bridge, threading its way between rocks in curves and meanders of its own design. For a moment I am lost in its leap and play, the fluid caress of water on stone. The river dances and shines in the spring light, and I am breathless before its rushing beauty. Light and water, water and light, dusting it with a thousand sparkles.

Sarita wiggles, and I am drawn back to my body, to motherhood and the child in my arms. She too is of the river, named for its leaping flow by older, distant generations who, like us, paused before its beauty. Sarita, they said in Sanskrit, referring to the flowing nature of life; Sarita, the river, in Hindi.

Keiran also had drawn his name from Hindi: *Kieran*, the ray of light, the spelling changed to combine Kelly and Anil. We had joined our children's names, like ourselves, to our origins in many worlds: Caribbean and American, Indian and European, father and mother, global and local. Water, I realize, water and light. Sarita and Keiran.

Absorbed in his own mysteries, Keiran has been inching toward the brook, until the tips of his boots rest in the water. Laughing, I take his hand, leading him into the stream, and he watches in fascination as the water flows over and around his boots, his feet safely dry. Only in the middle do I hoist him up, setting him down with a splash on the other side. Now reluctant to leave, he wades along the edge of the brook, heron-like, happily searching the shallows.

Giving him time to explore, I pause, looking upstream to the still waters of the marsh. A beaver dam has broadened and slowed its course, and it is beautiful in its quiet depth, the flush of green returning color to its banks. It is a scene I never tire of looking at, one I had photographed many times, the palette of seasons changing its hue. Nor was I the only one who appreciated its charm: I had found a black-and-white photo of it in Don's family album, labeled BROOK, 1918.

Nearly a hundred years later, the brook is surprisingly similar, the faded grays of the photograph transformed by spring into deep blues and greens. It is the same beautiful river, but now it is my family that stands at its banks, my children probing its mysteries of frog and mud. Watching Keiran's eager face peering into the river's immortal one, I feel our transience washing us downstream, sparkles of light on the water.

Holding Sarita more tightly, I call Keiran across the ford to a small ledge with space enough for three. The rocky outcropping offers a dry seat on the still soggy ground, and Keiran sits between us, his yellow boots stretched out in cheerful counterpoint to our practical black and brown ones. Sarita, as yet a mystery, lies peacefully in Anil's arms, her own particular enthusiasms still unknowable.

With my husband and two children beside me, I realize that our family is complete: There are no holes unfilled, no gaps of wanting. Now we can grow together, our vines twining around each other. For this moment, it is our home—our family—our farm—our story.

April 2010

Need!

The LAST days of April, and the strange early spring feels like an unusually early summer. Revolving in tight circles around Sarita, I am scarcely aware of the season's change, bound to more intimate cycles: nurse, change, rock, sleep (she more often than I), nurse again . . .

One day the sound of an engine penetrates my haze, and I look up, surprised to see Anil pushing the lawn mower past the window. I have not gone outside for days, nor, it seems, have I looked out the window, for I am startled to realize that the lawn is solidly green and leaves are pushing out from every twig.

Bemused, I gaze blankly, separated from reality by the strange detachment of sleep deprivation. Quietly dreamlike, Keiran appears in the window, a small man pushing a miniature lawn mower, the cheerful yellow of the mower matching his beloved boots. A white flash leaps behind him, then another, and I realize that the goats are once again on pasture. When I focus, I can see the whole herd spreading across the field. Overjoyed to be outside, they run twisting and kicking, momentarily mindless of the lush grass. Even the mature does leap in youthful exuberance, intoxicated by the fresh air.

Wishing to drink my own draught of such air, I push up the window, letting its freshness wash over me. With temperatures improbably in the 70s, we have abandoned the woodstove, and Sarita sleeps comfortably in her bassinet. Stretching, I welcome in spring—and, I realize, wrinkling my nose, the manure pile. All winter Anil had pitched the hog's manure outside the barn, where it lay, solidly frozen, without remark or offense. However, this unexpectedly warm spell has raised its temperature quickly, and, like a loaf of baking bread, it fills every corner with its distinctive aroma.

I groan to myself, hating to put one more task on Anil's shoulders, but there is no way around it; we will need to move it down to the fields—and soon. Other years we had left the goats' less-noisome bedding in the barn until we could clear it at our convenience. Without a tractor, we hauled it, cartload by cartload, through the fields, the precious daylight speeding by while the pen seemed to resist penetration.

Given the immensity of the task, we had turned all available—if reluctant—hands to the work, sending eager farm visitors into deeply piled pens, pitchforks in hand. Nephews and cousins, fresh from the city, poked tentatively at the caked manure, dubious of its purported value. Often it was midsummer before the bare boards appeared and we could wash down the floor, the thick sludge running out the cracks.

It is a huge and tedious task, and this year, without me, it is all his. With Keiran desperate to be outside, Anil decides to teach him the job. However, by mid-afternoon they are back, Keiran red-faced and Anil cranky.

"It will not work," Anil tells me. "The trek through the pasture is too difficult for him." With the already slow work dragged out to the point of no return, Anil looks at me in desperation. "We need a tractor!" he says, and although this is a constant phrase in our household, I know we are approaching a tipping point. Looking at his tired and frustrated face, I wonder, *Can we do this thing or not?*

Unwilling to give up, we realize that we only have one option: We will have to ask for help. Neil Peaslee, the local man who hays our field has, in his own words, "a tractor museum"—close to a hundred tractors in various states of functionality. Luckily, he has taken a liking to us, understanding our farm dreams from the inside out. When I put the situation to him—new baby and fragrant manure pile—he laughs, assuring us he will loan us a tractor for the weekend.

After a long and wakeful night, I come downstairs late Saturday morning to an empty house. Curious, I push open the garage door and see a blue tractor parked in our driveway, Keiran hovering around it in delight. It is an old machine, work-scarred, but one that we have seen in action. We only have it for one day, and there is a lot to be done, but we know it is battle-worthy.

Abandoning all other plans, I prepare myself to entertain both children, for, to Keiran's intense displeasure, Anil cannot take him on the tractor. Confined inside, Keiran heads for the window. Not to be denied, he climbs onto a high-back chair and watches intently as Anil navigates the tractor around the uneven ground, figuring out the best approach to the barn. The tractor, in unfamiliar hands, lurches as it digs at the steaming pile, then lifts its loaded bucket high.

Anil's slim young form looks strange on the tractor seat, accustomed as I am to the three local farmers—all double his age if not his weight. Relaxed and rounded at the wheel, they seem to flow into the tractor, shifting from man to machine as naturally as a centaur turns from man to horse. In vivid contrast, my young husband, straight and alert at the wheel, seems liable to spring from the seat at any moment.

However, experience counts more than energy, and Anil drives at a snail's speed, to Keiran's surprised displeasure. His return trip is faster, and he maneuvers the bucket more smoothly, getting a feel for the controls. Threading a path between barn and field, he takes trip after trip, and the pile dwindles—slowly to Keiran, but gratifyingly fast to me. Still, naptime arrives before Anil is finished, and I wrench Keiran away from the window with promises of a ride later that afternoon. Coming downstairs, I see Anil opening the door, grinning with the satisfaction of a job well done.

"We need a tractor," he repeats.

Nor is Anil the only one in desperate need of a tractor; Keiran moons around the window all afternoon, looking longingly at the battered machine.

"Blue tractor," he repeats, again and again, adoringly, "*Peasee* blue tractor."

Later in the week, with only toys at his disposal, he resorts to driving his red tractor back and forth on the window ledge.

"Dada driving," he tells me. "Pig poop!"

MAY 2010

PLANTING

MAY, OH SWEET MAY! Overnight, it seems, the leaves have opened, and, looking out, I can see only green. Not yet settled into the stolid sameness of midlife, the leaves pulse with every shade and hue, surrounding us with a fluttering, dappled sea of green. The bent form of the hawthorn is suddenly youthful again, leaves softening her limbs, flower buds swollen. Only the birds remember her age, perching on her dead branches and chattering of years gone by. The apple trees surge with desire, impatient for pollination. One day I show Keiran their pink-tinged buds hidden among the leaves. The next, the tree is adorned in white, her flowers spread wide, a waiting bride. Petals blow on the road like snow, and Keiran scoops them up in his shovel, delighted.

The river too is transformed, and we listen with delight to the urgent chattering of her guests. Sudden host to a frenzy of spring desire, her banks overflow with seasonal visitors intent on bringing forth new life. The red-winged blackbirds swarm back and forth from the marsh to the feeders, their wing bars reddening as the females arrive. A pair of

Canadian geese, defending their nests, honk in indignation at the bold advances of single geese, testing their commitment.

In the evening, the spring peepers dominate the airwaves. The voices of each miniature frog join in a single, sweetly deafening chorus, as if the marsh itself were a violin, vibrating with amphibious desire. Standing in the back door, I feel the rhythmic swell of their voices rising from the brook, engulfing me, body and soul, in the fullness of spring.

As the days lengthen, the quality of the light changes, lingering softly golden, reluctant to depart. Keiran protests as I put him to bed, convinced that it is not yet time to rest. The light pools on his floor in temptation, mocking the heavy curtains I hang in futile dissuasion. Confronted with the apparently absurd, he watches at the window longingly when I leave, despite my assurance that he needs energy for gardening in the morning.

Descending the stairs, I hear the whip-poor-will begin its nightly refrain, calling to Keiran through the open window. *Whip-poor-will, whip-poor-will, whip-poor-will*, it cries in relentless temptation, reminding him of delights denied.

But morning offers its own reward, dawning bright and clear, summoning us outside. With the ground warming quickly, it is urgent that we transplant the onions and plant the potatoes. Luckily, the slight breeze is sufficient to keep the blackflies at bay, and we head to the garden with high spirits, seedling trays in hand. While I pull up the black plastic, exposing the rich soil, Keiran digs in the soft dirt, looking for worms. Spying one, he cries out in excitement, bending over to pick it up.

"Nice wormy," he says, cradling it carefully in his palm, remembering what I have told him about their role in the garden.

"Yes, Keiran," I explain, smiling. "The worms help our garden. They turn compost into dirt. Earth," I tell him, filling his hands with the rich loam.

He listens quietly, examining the soil. Bending, he scoops up his own handful of dirt, offering it back to me.

Carefully, I pick out the weeds and rocks, cradling his hands around the soft dirt.

"This is food for the plants—earth," I continue, and watch his face, so intent and open.

What do we teach our children? I wonder. *How do we instill in them a sense of wonder and responsibility? Will he grow to hate this work, this slow bending of back, tired of the dirt and worms that now enthrall him? For now he shadows us, eager to share our knowledge, our work his play. When does it become work?*

I smile then, amused by my own conclusions, for farming *is* still a delight for Anil and me, even when it is most hard. Bending over the tray of onion seedlings, we smile at each other in anticipation—time to plant!

I mix compost into the topsoil, then trace a thin line in the dirt with the edge of my hoe. Fascinated, he watches as I separate out the individual plants, their tiny roots briefly exposed. Quickly I tuck them into the ground, pulling the supporting soil around their tiny forms. Their stems, so robust in the seedling tray, disappear as we plant them in the ground, as insubstantial as blades of grass.

He looks dubiously at the row we've planted, their green stems barely visible, and I laugh, reassuring him, "Wait until summer when they've had a chance to grow. Then you can dig them up." Digging he knows, and, with the faith of experience, he smiles, running back to the potatoes waiting in the shade.

Our seed potatoes had arrived a few weeks earlier, and we had stored them in the cool darkness of the basement, trying to suppress their urge to grow. However, when I open the bags, I can see that they have already sent out long, pale shoots, determinedly seeking the sun.

Knowing our garden space is limited this year, I leave small potatoes whole, cutting the rest into generous pieces. Keiran watches in fascination as I split the potatoes, their dusty skins opening to reveal yellow or red or purplish blue. He touches them gently, fingers seeking eyes, and I am reminded of Beth and her lifelong fascination with potatoes.

Beth and I had joked about her getting a "tuber grant" to write a book, imagining her traveling the world with a dusty notebook, chronicling the stories of the humble spud, earth-dweller extraordinaire. We knew—even then—that our journey would be brief, and we laughed at our boundless dreams, knowing we would need many lifetimes for all our excursions. Still, the world was magnificent and our curiosity insatiable, and so we kept our horizons broad.

Now, however, the harsh light of reality was melting our dreams, and it was hard to keep despair from filling its void. For Beth, at least, the wonders of life were receding, her book still unwritten.

Looking at Keiran next to me, I know I can offer him no more than this: the gift of curiosity, of life engaged, each day precious. Together we push our shovels into the ground, making room for the new plants to grow. I show him how to place the potato, eyes up to look for the sun, carefully drawing the dirt over it.

At first he is reluctant to part with his seed pieces, watching dubiously as they disappear into the earth. Bending down to plant some more, I call for a potato with no response, and straighten up to see him digging up the first piece. Understanding his concern at their disappearance, I assure him that the plant will soon send new shoots out of the soil. Trusting me, he follows me down the row, and together we plant the next generation.

While Keiran naps, I plan a brief foray outside with Sarita, eager to share some of spring's delight with my daughter. The thermometer reads 78, promising the comfort of midsummer, but Sarita's skin, newly minted, burns easily, so I wrap her in a blanket to cover her tiny limbs.

As we step out from the coolness of the house, the sunlight pours over us in a warm waterfall, and I tip my face up in welcome. Sarita, affronted by the relentless cascade of light, squirms and grunts, squinting her eyes tightly shut. I shift, casting my own shadow over her, and sidle sideways toward the stone bench like a determined crab. The stone is warm, inviting, and I half expect to see lizards basking. Instead, we are joined by Diego, who sprawls in delight next to us, stretching to his full length.

My small daughter soon squalls her displeasure at the sun's continued assault, and I rise, seeking deeper shade. Jiggling her in my arms, I head for the hawthorn tree. Commonly known as the May-tree, it had been the inspiration for Sarita's middle name, and it seems fitting that it should protect her now. Shielded from the sun, she quiets, her dark eyes opening wide. As she relaxes, so can I, and I slowly become aware of a strong scent, sweet and wild like cherry blossoms. Looking up, I realize that the hawthorn flowers, only buds this morning, have fully opened.

The tree, in full bloom, is indeed a "May Queen," its white flowers redolent with perfume. Perhaps at a distance it could suggest spiritual purity, as the church claimed, but, in the perfumed embrace of its boughs, I am reminded of older, more natural celebrations: the return of fertility and the rise of new life. A bee crawls across its petals, and, following its ascent into the heart of the tree, I am suddenly gazing into another world. Hundreds of bees—millions of bees—hang suspended above my head, like dust motes caught in the golden sun. A low buzz emanates from the canopy, as if the tree itself were singing, humming with the energy of photosynthesis and the flow of sap to new green leaves.

Quiet in my arms, Sarita stares, entranced, black eyes into white blooms, washed in a humming bath of color and scent. Life, it seems, has returned to Hewett Road.

MAY 2010

PASSAGE

THE END of May, and the thermometer reads an unbelievable 100.9. Inside with the children, I close windows only recently opened, trying to stop the heat from penetrating the cool sanctuary of the house. Pulling the heavy curtains, I sink the living room into a strange twilight, but the air slowly thickens and boils, and Keiran cries without knowing why. Sarita sleeps for hours, her small body sprawled on the sheet, surfacing only to nurse.

At naptime I check the garden, the sunlight glaring white against the wilting plants. The peas hang their heads, no longer stretching up the trellis, and lettuce huddles against the ground in futile escape. The transplanted onions have almost melted under the oppressive heat, their thin stems shrunken. Even the vigorous garlic shows the strain, the tips of their leaves browning. The air itself seems to burn, acrid with smoke from massive forest fires in Quebec, hundreds of miles to the north. Heeding air-quality warnings, I duck back into the house, grateful for the relief from the sun if not the heat.

When Keiran wakes, I hustle the children into the car, thankful for the brief respite of air-conditioning. Despite the horrendous temperatures, we cannot find sanctuary at home: Beth is rapidly losing her battle, and we have been advised to visit as soon as possible. Stopping only to pick Anil up at work, we head to her house, disbelief warring with dread. Good-byes do not seem possible, and I choke on stifled tears, not wanting to frighten the children.

I park next to her garden, now visible only in memory, tall weeds erasing any hint of its previous bounty. Braced by my family, I knock and enter, stepping into the familiar house with its years of memories, now transformed, threatened.

Beth sits waiting on the corner of a borrowed hospital bed, her shoulders high and squared, holding herself inside their protective guards. She turns toward me stiffly, imprisoned by the pain that radiates from her taut skin. Still, she is Beth, her spirit indomitable, and somehow she manages a smile and a glad, if faint, "Kelly!," as if I had made her day, as if anything could penetrate her pain.

Beth was famous for her greetings, for the sincerely exuberant cry with which she met your entrance, as if you alone brought life and joy into the room. Normally it was a leaping embrace of the spirit, almost physical in its force, but now it whispered out, echoing in memory alone.

Gently I slip into her proffered arms, kiss her cheek, wishing I could warm her with my love in return. She is almost pure spirit now, her body so wasted that she feels hollow in my arms, an empty milkweed pod, bound to the stalk after the downy seeds have flown. Her face, etched with pain, is almost unrecognizable. She has defied death for a long time, but at a terrible cost, bound to the gray world of painkillers.

Keiran cries, confused by the changes in his friend, so Anil carries him outside, retreating into the cool dimness of the forest. I sit next to Beth, lightly resting my head on her shoulder, but visible pain washes over her, and I realize she is denied even the comfort of touch.

Sitting up, I slide across from her, looking at her beloved face.

"Do you remember . . . ?" I begin, walking backwards with her, seeking solace in memories. For a moment, the past is more real than the present, and she reaches out of her pain to finish the stories, remembering the laughter of midnight jokes, the beauty of the desert in bloom.

For a moment she surfaces, but she is almost gone, consumed by pain, and finally she staggers to the table, loading herself up with more painkillers. Easing herself back to her bed, she is quiet, eyes closed, and I settle Sarita to nurse, absorbed as always in her eager sucking. Lifting her up to burp, I realize that Beth is watching her, the small urgency of her life reaching through the haze of medication. I turn Sarita to face Beth, and she hums like a large bee, her vocalizations on a primal plane of vibration.

"She sounds like an airplane," Beth says, and I laugh, glad for their connection. Unaware of pain, Sarita looks back at her, black eyes into black eyes, knowing only the allure of spirit.

It is dark when we return home, and I flip on the floodlight, illuminating the garden.

The plants are strangely colorless, shades of black and gray, their shapes strangely one-dimensional, thin shadows of themselves. The soil is parched, and as I water the garden, the smell of the earth rises around me, thirsty for more. Lightning flashes on the horizon, but no rain comes to break the heat, and Sarita sweats in her crib. She wakes every few hours, crying, but turns away from my full breast, milk leaking onto her cheek.

A few days later we are called to Beth's side for a final parting. Her hospital room is filled with people, but she seems unaware of us, making her passage alone. She breathes loudly, visibly, and I feel the great gift that binds us—life in, life out, the shared breath of dinosaurs and pharaohs, algae and elephants, friends and family. For a few minutes more we share life, sweet and painful life, and I lay my hand open on hers, feeling the strength of her long fingers, artist's fingers, creators of beauty.

"I'm here," I tell her, but I think she knows, our atoms joined by love.

On the drive home, I rest my head on the window, looking out with the quiet detachment of loss. Life parades before me, life minus one, yet I see her everywhere I look. A young woman stoops in her garden, intent on some urgent weeding. An old woman walks her dog, taking care of daily needs. The billboard of a local diner cheerily boasts, "Home cooking so good you'll think we kidnapped your mama." All the mundane activities of everyday life shine with their own existence. "Here we are," they proclaim. "Here we are."

That night, Sarita is restless, and I pull her bassinet next to our bed, glad for the excuse to keep her close. She cries frequently, and I reach in, resting my hand on her back. Through her sleeper I can feel the rapid beat of her heart, the insistent pulsing of life.

"I'm here baby, I'm here," I tell her, soothing, the warmth of my open palm pressing into her. She grunts in her sleep like a small animal, settling.

Here. We. Are.

PART IV

SUMMER:
THE POSSIBILITIES
OF RIPENESS

June 2010

Rain

THE FIRST of June brings rain and cooler temperatures, a return to normal spring weather. I watch the garden through the window, the soil darkening as it accepts the water, the plants swelling as they drink.

"Rain, rain, go away," Keiran chants, gleeful to have mastered an appropriate rhyme, so I correct him gently. "No, Keiran, we need the rain; the plants are thirsty."

He listens, studying the garden, the thick new leaves of the potato bed visible from his bedroom window.

"Butterfly," he says in sudden delight, and I look up to see a tiger swallowtail on the lilacs, its yellow-and-black wings vivid against the dull gray skies.

Although life continues with its usual intensity, my own grief lingers, blurring the borders of reality. Uneasy in sleep, I dream that I have forgotten my children in the car or found them crying in a broken-down crib. I move in a stupor, sleepwalking, raising my head in surprise to find myself in the wrong place at the wrong time.

Late one afternoon I find myself in front of the sink, staring in surprise at a slab of pig belly. That morning I had taken what I thought was a chicken out of the freezer, planning to roast it whole. Thawing, however, had apparently wrought miraculous—if undesirable—transformations, and the meat before me was undeniably porcine. Pig belly, with its densely packed layers of meat and fat, was normally reserved for bacon in Western cuisine. Lacking the time to make bacon, we had frozen the belly intact, with some vague notion that it was favored in Chinese cooking. Anil, with his typical confidence, had dared to cook some freehand, but even the love of a wife could not find much appeal in the stubbornly tough cubes of meat.

With recipes as yet unexplored, the pig belly lies in the sink in defiance of culinary appeal.

"I guess we have no dinner tonight," I announce to the empty kitchen.

Frustrated at having my plans thwarted, I turn on the water for pasta, our last defense against hunger. While the noodles boil, I steal glances at the slab of meat, still surprised by its presence. What am I to do with it? Drained by grief, I barely have the energy to cook, much less embark on a research project. Still, what else can I do? I cannot waste the pig's life, offered up so generously in my sink.

Bringing out a stack of cookbooks, I search their indexes, leafing through possible recipes. There are not a lot of options, but at last I pause, considering the two-page spread before me. *Braised Pork Belly*,[1] it proclaims, the glossy photo showing neat cubes of meat, browned to crispy succulence. The recipe, however, requires two days to complete, and I close the book rather emphatically, its large pages thumping shut in indignation.

Cleaning up after dinner, I am confronted once again by the offending meat, blocking the sink. I cannot discard it, and so, reluctantly, I reopen the cookbook. The first step is to make a brine to tenderize and flavor the meat overnight. Except for the ample amount of kosher salt, our garden has all the major ingredients—rosemary, thyme, parsley, and garlic—a fact which gives me intense satisfaction.

During my footloose years as a single woman, I had longed for an herb garden, and, when I finally settled, they were some of the first plants I set out. In the chaos of new motherhood, when all was abandoned, the herbs had forgiven my neglect and persisted, even thrived. Now, as I harvest their luxuriant growth, I am bathed in their pungent odors, evoking powerful memories.

Traditionally, rosemary signifies remembrance, and as I drop the stalks into my basket, it is not a long way to thoughts of Beth. Indeed, as I return to the kitchen, it's as if she comes in with me, laughing at the unexpected gift of the pig belly, turning my frustrated despair into creative hope. This was her particular art—not alchemy, but belief—seeing the connections the rest of us overlooked.

Tying back my hair, I smell the herbs' spicy perfumes on my fingers. I too am steeped in life, pungent and rich, and so I cook with Beth beside me, connecting farm and family.

Engaged in the slow process of food preparation, I have time to consider the impact our farm has had on our families, our extended pumpkin vine of friends and relatives. Although the beauty of our land has nearly universal appeal, not everyone likes being reminded of their connection to their food. Although Anil's siblings are accustomed to home butchering, his niece, raised mostly in the United States, had rarely been exposed to it. An avowed animal lover, she nonetheless used to relish goat curry—until she witnessed a goat being butchered at our farm. Now she refuses to eat goat altogether.

I laugh in amusement, wondering if our farm is having a positive impact. Still, we have served a purpose: Our guests now eat with awareness, knowing the price their appetite has exacted. This, I conclude, is not a bad thing. While some of our friends eat meat with a more-restrained appetite, others offer their help at slaughtering time. Alex and Kathy, ambivalent at first, later asked us to raise a pig for them, so they could experience eating the whole hog—and make soap from its lard!

I am glad that we can share the reality of farm life with so many people; it is too special—and in today's world, too rare—an experience not to share. Soon our annual round of summer visitors would begin again, bringing their worlds to circle around us. Our pumpkin vines had grown long, pulling family together from Tennessee to Texas, with roots reaching to Trinidad and St. Marten, Spain, Lebanon, and the Philippines.

The children of the family are cheerful mixes of culture and custom, derivatives of color-blind love, brought forth with great hope. Quintessentially American, they are also global citizens, at home with a far-flung family. For even if extended, we *are* undeniably family, comfortably chaotic, our single small bathroom pulling us together for tooth-brushing parties. My kitchen would soon smell of lemon and garlic, or soy sauce and ginger, and meals would appear on our dining room table, tangible expressions of love and culture.

Reflecting on the cheerful chaos that will soon ensue, I smile at Anil as he comes in from chores, his dark hair damp from the rain.

"I hope our guests like pig belly," I say, indicating the slab of meat, now almost enticing in its dressing of herbs.

He looks at it with interest, regarding the long layers of meat and fat, the darkened brine. Child of a sociable culture, he enjoys the noisy bustle of visitors and takes pride in sharing the farm with them. Still, he also remembers the demands of hosting, and knows we will soon have very little time alone.

"Come look at the animals, like old times," he says, and I tuck the meat into the fridge, hoping for the best.

In the darkness, the slight drizzle is refreshing, and I turn my face up to its gentle kiss. It is peaceful walking beside him through the night, and I dare to dream of the farm fully tended and growing with intention. Taking my hand, he leads me through the darkened corridor to the new pigpen he has built.

Rhodora had grown into a massive hog, only her legs still improbably small. Now, disturbed from her sleep, she regards us with annoyance. Our hands entwined, Anil and I stand close, happy, and I laugh at the setting of our romance. My father used to invite my mother to walk up to the garden, and my brothers and I would giggle, as if the garden were an excuse for intimacy. Too young to understand the joy of a shared dream, we did not see the delight of the garden itself.

Here, in company with a disgruntled sow, Anil and I find contentment. In our happiness, we do not forget Beth; we hold each other's hands tighter in remembrance. With the past surrounding us and our dreams leading us on, we savor the present and our joy in each other.

NOTE

1. Thomas Keller, *Ad Hoc at Home* (New York: Artisan, 2009).

June 2010

The Wild

L ATE JUNE, and we arrive at the summer solstice. We teeter on the edge of darkness and light, then land with a soft sigh, pushed into summer. The gradual retreat of the light should be a bitter pill, but we swallow it with little protest, lulled by the length of days. In our electrified world, few remember our obedience to celestial cycles or our placement in the natural world. Now, with loss haunting me, the solstice reminds me of Beth, her celebrations inviting us to remember our connections.

It is hot this side of summer, and hazy, the sky neither blue nor gray. Keiran stays close to the stroller as we walk, his usual exuberant gallop curtailed. Only one day in, but it feels and looks like midsummer. The trees, fully leafed, create a solid green wall framing the pasture. The field itself is dotted with flowers, clover and vetch, buttercups and daisies, but it is a muted palette, splashes of purple, yellow, and white that do not disturb the eye. The grasses, given over to maturity, bend heavy with seeds.

A turkey head bobs up from the tall grass, then sinks back, evading notice. It is a marked contrast from the spring, when the toms had staggered in drunken display after great bands of hens, careless as dinosaurs. Now the boldness of courtship had yielded to the caution of maternity, and I realize they must be surrounded by their young. In previous years, walking through the field, I had waded unknowing into turkey families, the chicks leaping before me in fluttering panic. Now, surrounded by my own young, I am confined to the road, and the turkeys are left in peace, their invisibility maintained.

Hardly past our property line, I realize Keiran is suffering in the 90-degree heat. Like a wilting plant, he walks, head down, his two hands attached to the stroller.

"Do you want to walk some more or turn around?" I ask him. For the first time I can remember, he chooses retreat. "Turn around," he says, pushing on the stroller wheels in his haste.

I spread a blanket under an old apple tree, the temperature more bearable in the shade. Sarita lies open-limbed, her body abandoned to the heat, her dark eyes fastened on the leaves above. Keiran makes short forays to a pile of wood chips, fascination forcing him out of the shade, heat pushing him back. Eventually he settles for arranging his tools against the stroller, evaluating the leverage of the hoe versus the shovel, the weight of the metal rake versus the bamboo. Diego slides into the shade without a sound, and I turn to find him sprawled full-length next to Sarita, his body as long as hers.

I point out the small green apples that have replaced the blossoms of spring, and Keiran begs me to pick one, excited by the miniature fruit. Since most will drop uneaten, I select a few of the choicest ones. He holds them tightly, refusing to put any down, until his arms round with his treasure.

"Baby apple," he repeats at intervals, showing them to me proudly, and I am amazed at the clarity of his speech, remembering his refrain of *Ap, ap* only last fall.

A prolonged rustling in the bushes makes me turn around, expecting to see our other cat, Jade, but the leaves part to reveal a wilder companion. A young porcupine stares back at me, its small eyes dark and glistening.

Calling Keiran to me, I point it out, and he immediately pushes against my restraining arms, irresistibly attracted to any baby.

"Keiran pat it," he implores, seeking release.

I laugh, having forgotten how new he still is to the world. *This* baby, I explain, is not soft or delicate. His eyes never leaving it, he tries again, hopefully. "Mama pat it?"

The porcupine, having finished its own assessment, turns away, its hind quills splayed in defense like an irritable peacock. Despite its comical waddle, it moves quickly across the lawn, then turns into the taller pasture grass and vanishes, a rapidly retreating rustle in the grass. Watching it so easily disappear, I wonder what other denizens of the wild pass by unnoticed.

Although I knew the wild surrounded us, it was easy to forget until it walked across our doorstep. A few weeks earlier, I had chanced to spy a moose grazing in the brook. Although aware there were moose around, we had never seen one, and I had stared in disbelief at the large brown lump in the brook. Only when it lifted up its long neck and head, removing all doubt of its moosie-ness, had I called excitedly to our guests, a Jamaican-Italian couple.

We had clustered at the back door, passing around an old pair of binoculars. Through its lens, I could see that it was a cow, tall and—for a moose—rather delicate. As if sensing our gaze, the cow had turned, looking directly at us, then moved toward the bank, gaining speed. Pulling herself onto solid ground, she was suddenly all legs. To my surprise, she was graceful and swift, rapidly crossing the field and disappearing into the woods.

So quickly was she gone that I had watched a few minutes more, wondering what else I had missed. It seemed ludicrous that such a large beast could remain largely invisible to us. Were we really so blind? Our ancestors, in all parts of the globe, knew their environment intimately: the signs of animal passage, the predictors of weather, even the movement of stars. Now, no longer directly reliant on nature for survival, we had lost most of that awareness. It seemed a sad, and dangerous, loss—not to know our placement within the whole of nature. What beauty we were missing, what sense of wonder?

That evening, dark eyes shining, Keiran tells Anil about the porcupine.

Sharing his delight, Anil lingers at Keiran's bedside, reluctant to break the spell. However, reminded of the wild, Anil finally whispers, "I think I'll go for a paddle—it's now or never."

I nod at him silently, knowing this is true—that the pace of summer will only quicken. "Be careful," I whisper, for it is twilight, and he will be alone on the water.

He grins at me, teasing; the brook is shallow, and the aluminum canoe, with its heavy, broad belly, almost unsinkable.

With plenty to do, I do not realize how much time has passed until Anil opens the door to the kitchen, letting in the cool night air. He is grinning, radiant with the mystery of the wild, and it is only as he enters that I realize he is dripping, soaked from head to foot. Ignoring my concern, he shrugs and laughs.

"You missed the birds," he says, eager to share his discoveries.

As he paddled out, he had startled several families of ducks, their babies bumping into each other in comically hurried retreat. Slowing, he had idled in the water, letting the boat float where it would. Given free rein, the brook had deposited him in a clump of marsh grass, and there the night creatures had forgotten him.

Slowly, as if waking, the landscape had begun to move, its inhabitants once again busy about their lives. The dark shadow of an owl separated from a tree, passing overhead on soundless wings. Farther down, a small animal swam across the river, the ball of its head proceeding resolutely across the channel. Too distant to see clearly, it was nonetheless identifiable by its action: a beaver carrying twigs!

Although there were two old lodges in the brook, we had never seen or heard beaver activity. Excited by this sign of life, Anil had slid the canoe quietly downriver and nestled it alongside the lodge. He swung his foot out onto the grassy bank, expecting to meet solid ground, but his foot plunged instead straight down, deep into the cool water. Startled, he grabbed the gunwales, tipping the boat—and himself—fully into the river's embrace.

Upright again, he laughed, relieved to find himself (only!) in waist-deep water. Already wet, he took the opportunity to examine the lodge closely, looking for signs of use. However, it cleverly concealed its inner life, and eventually he pulled the boat onto the bank, wetter if not wiser.

It was, in its own way, a nocturnal baptism, a tactile reminder of our place within the natural world. Wading in the chilly water, Anil was simply one more soggy animal, scrambling for dry ground. As he tells me the story, stripping off his wet clothes, he is suddenly vulnerable—if laughing—and I wonder what other animals prowled the marsh at night. Now armed with a towel, he rubs his hair into a thickly springing black pelt, and I am reminded of another nighttime adventure.

Arriving home late after a scorching summer day, we had headed out with flashlights to water the garden. The lights, flitting across garden beds and wilting plants, revealed an unexpected sight: Worms, hundreds of them, lay stretched out to unbelievable lengths across the soil. Many were twined together, their casual tangle belying the intimacy of their embrace.

Astonished, I stood and stared. I could not believe their incredible size, their prodigious numbers, or the boldness of their location—as if a whole civilization had been concealed in my familiar garden. I reached out with curious fingers, seeking the confirmation of touch. However, at my slightest touch, they sprang back, shrinking to normal plump wormi-ness. Laughing now, I walked my fingers down the row, leaving a trail of shrunken and terrorized worms. Heading inside, amused, I realized they must be night crawlers.

Apparently it is not just individuals we miss; there are whole worlds beneath our feet. On a farm, surrounded by plants and animals, we think ourselves familiars of the natural world. However, nature is deeper and broader than our domesticated realm, and she cradles us in a wild embrace.

Strange noises waken me, our open windows letting in the cries of night wanderers. Lying still, listening, I realize I do not know their language.

"What was that?" I ask the darkness, but Anil sleeps peacefully next to me, not wired to mother-alarms, and the wild moves on unnamed.

July 2010

Tractor

THE CALENDAR declares that time, reliably, has brought us into July, but I cannot shake the slightly breathless feeling that we have fast-forwarded into the future. Unbelievably, we have decided to buy a tractor! Not in five years, or next year, but now, in the very immediate present.

After five years of paperwork and dedication, Anil had finally been granted American citizenship. Ever supportive, my parents had attended his naturalization ceremony in Portland, and afterwards, given him their own gift. Although they were continually amazed by Anil's ability to "make something out of nothing," they knew he could only accomplish so much on evenings and weekends. If we still wanted a tractor, they told us, they would help to make a down payment.

Help? Want? We laughed in disbelief—it *was* a gift substantial enough to make a difference. Could we really own a tractor—now? For a month we agonized over our decision. Could we afford another monthly payment? Was it wise to deplete our already small safety cushion? Yet it also seemed foolish not to make this step; how else could we seriously start to build our business, constrained as we were by labor?

For weeks we consider what we really need in a tractor. Since the dairy will be our commercial enterprise, we prioritize the needs of the goats over the garden. Putting aside thoughts of a plow, we talk buckets, first and foremost—nothing slows us down as much as cleaning pens by hand!

We have also been warned that it is easy to outgrow one's tractor, so we discuss our long-term plans, trying to figure out how large an engine we really need. For now we will only pull a bush hog to mow the fields as we rotate the goats through the pasture. Eventually, though, we hope to harvest our own hay, and will need the horsepower to pull a baler. The smallest tractor that could handle such a load, we are told, is 45 horsepower.

Whereas the specifics of the tractor require great thought, there is surprisingly little discussion over which brand to buy. Although Keiran is fixated on John Deere tractors, this time it is Anil who will be the driver, and he is most familiar with Kubotas. Nor do we consider a used tractor. Given our limited time, we cannot spend it on repairs—we need to get right to work!

Having told Keiran that we are going to buy a tractor, we wait until we have reinforcements to go to the store. While we fill out a credit application, Keiran cruises the lineup of tractors with Alex and Kathy. With Sarita asleep in my arms, we are quickly absorbed in asking our own questions. We need to decide on specific features—Whether to load our tires with "beet juice"? Hydrostatic or not? Type of tread?—so we listen carefully, already starting to feel like tractor owners.

Hearing feet shuffling behind me, I turn to see Keiran in Alex's arms, watching us intently.

"What did you see?" I ask him, and his face is instantly transformed.

"BIG Ku-bo-ta!" he exclaims, delight audible in every syllable. The salesman looks up from his paperwork, and we joke about using Keiran for advertisements.

After a few more questions, the salesman shakes our hands, sealing the deal; as long as our credit is approved, we'll have a tractor in a few weeks. Despite the firmness of his handshake, it is hard to believe that we are—almost—the proud owners of a tractor.

On Monday I answer each phone call expectantly, but none concerns the tractor. Tuesday I take the children for an early morning walk, and the answering machine blinks promisingly when we return. The message is hopeful: Our credit has been approved, and they have found the model we want in a neighboring state. They will pick up the tractor on Wednesday and will begin modifications. "Soon," the salesman promises as I replay the message, "you will have it soon."

After such anticipation, the arrival of the tractor is, for me, anticlimactic.

Sarita, usually so peaceful, has been twisting and turning in some inner distress, unable to sleep. Only my presence calms her, so I sit in her darkened room, endlessly soothing. When Anil pokes his head in to tell me the tractor has arrived, I shrug helplessly, motioning him to go. Frustrated by my own fetters, I am yet more distressed by Sarita's crying, and cannot leave her alone.

When she finally quiets, I sneak a peek out the window. I see the tractor immediately, its brilliant orange glowing in the midday sun. Keiran is already in the driver's seat, Anil's hand safely on his back, and Don stands next to them, nodding his head.

Don has shared our excitement over the new tractor, asking about its arrival every day, so Anil has invited him over to check it out. Now, hearing Sarita's cries once again ringing out, the two men look up.

"It looks great!" Don calls to me, the approval of a practical man looking at a well-forged tool.

It is twilight when Anil comes in, and I can tell that he is pleased.

"Come," he says, smiling, "look out the bedroom window."

Following him slowly upstairs, I search for enthusiasm underneath my crushing fatigue, but I do not need to pretend when I see his work. He has cut a long path through the field connecting our house to the brook, making it easier for me to walk with the kids. It is not the most important task, but it is heartening to see how much he can do with the tractor—and it will help my spirits to get back into the fields.

I know that the tractor will be there tomorrow—and the next day— and I will have a chance to make its acquaintance, this feat of engineering that promises so much. Sitting in the driveway, it is hope made concrete, giving us the help we so desperately need to revive the farm. The tractor will wait, but my daughter will not. As she gains her footing and finds her place on the farm, I will measure her growth against its sides, until one day she too can drive it.

The next day Sarita is still fussy, so I lie next to her on the mattress, comforting her. When she finally sleeps, she sinks into a deep repose, and I follow her under, relieved. For hours we lie there, reassured by the rumble of the tractor, all of life busy around our quiet island.

When we finally come downstairs, the house is empty, although I know guests will be arriving soon. Hearing the ripping of corn husks, I head for the screened-in porch, knowing my mother must be busy. Despite being the victim of a horrific car accident, which had left permanent physical and mental injuries, she has maintained a cheerful and generous spirit, and can always be counted on to lend the first hand.

Since Sarita's birth, she had often stayed with us, cleaning, cooking, and entertaining Keiran. It was by no means easy for her to help us, and yet she persisted patiently, knowing *her* little girl needed help. Watching her shucking the corn, I breathe in her strength and courage. I too can make it through.

She looks up, smiling, as we join her. While I settle in to feed Sarita, she fills me in on the events of the day. Our guests had indeed arrived, but they were all outside, keeping the tractor busy. After Anil had cleaned the pigpen, he had given rides to Keiran and his cousins on the (now fragrant!) tractor. It is rather breathtaking to hear her tell it so calmly—the pen cleaned so easily, and still time to play—as if it were all in a normal day's work.

The next morning Sarita is finally relaxed, and I hand her off to eager relatives. Now that we have a tractor payment, I am even more determined to save our pennies, so I bypass the clothes dryer and slip outside to hang the laundry. The tractor glows invitingly in the morning light, and I pause, basket in hand, to admire it. I ease up to it shyly, shifting the laundry to my hip so that I can run my hand down its solid flanks.

It is much lower than Don's John Deere, an easy step up, and I hesitate just a minute before setting down the laundry.

Feeling like a naughty child, I climb onto the shiny new seat and settle behind the wheel. Although I have driven a few other tractors—and I fully intend to drive this one!—I lack mechanical confidence, and I gaze in some bafflement at all the controls. There seem to be a lot more than I remember, but I know I will soon master them. Stranded in PARK for now, I settle for turning the wheel, hoping nobody is watching.

July 2010

Milestones

THE LAST day of July has arrived, and with it Keiran's second birthday. I wake early, knowing we have a lot to do in preparation for his party. Later I will have time to reflect on his growth in the past year, but for now there is work to do.

I tiptoe downstairs, trying to be quiet, but our house is full of visiting family, and it is hard to navigate through all of the makeshift beds.

Anil, Alex, and Albert assemble in the kitchen, rumpled but grinning, while I make coffee. The Three As, we call them, for they are truly amigos, brothers not only in law, but in their deep love of nature. Born in different parts of the globe,[1] they now live on opposite sides of the country, but their connections far outweigh any differences.

This morning they share an important job: to slaughter a goat for the party. Home butchering is now a natural part of our celebrations, requiring only a quick check that we have enough freezer bags. All of the men are experienced at the task, and their talk turns to the exceptional and comical. Their laughter wakes Brandon, relegated, as the teenage cousin,[2] to the couch, and he joins us in the kitchen in search of sustenance.

Born and raised in comfortable suburbia, Brandon had chosen, twice, to volunteer his help on our farm. Still, at fifteen, his inexperience is fresh on his sleepy face, and the men watch him thoughtfully as he joins their talk. Substituting youthful bravado for experience, he boasts about his love of meat, describing his favorite cuts in enthusiastic detail.

Albert, irrepressible, claps Brandon on the shoulder.

"You should help us," he says. "It would be good for you!"

Anil only watches, grinning, but Alex chimes in, encouraging. "It's not as bad as you would expect."

Equal parts meat lover *and* animal lover, Brandon hesitates, but his adolescent pride wins, and he joins them with apparent nonchalance.

With hostess duties keeping me inside, I watch them go, wondering what Brandon will make of the experience. His return to the farm had been a surprise, as we hadn't thought he enjoyed the work. Two years earlier he had come to "test his muscles," but had found many things offensive, particularly the smell and the heat. As he pulled cartload after cartload of manure, he groaned that we were killing him, despite his growing strength.

We had given him other chores that he enjoyed more—taming some skittish goats, watering the garden—but we hadn't expected him to return. For children more attuned to computers than nature, farm life was a foreign world, demanding a different set of skills and paying a more subtle reward. So when he asked to come back, we were as surprised as we were pleased, wondering what quiet magic the farm had worked.

This time we had decided to let him select his own activities. To our delight, he chose one of our top-priority projects, the renovation of the milk room. Although the room had not been cleaned in several decades, Don had used it as his milk room, and the floor—albeit cracked—was the requisite concrete. Even the milk inspector had seen the promise beneath the years of neglect, reassuring us that it would not be difficult to restore.

However, a year had passed since the inspector's visit, and we had made no progress, handicapped as usual by lack of time. Knowing that having two extra hands around was a rare opportunity, I had immediately put Brandon to work. To safely process milk, everything had to be clean and sterile, so floor, walls, even the ceiling, needed to be scrubbed. Once washed, the walls were lighter but still dingy, so Brandon set to work, carefully brushing paint onto the rough blocks.

With a fresh coat of white paint, the room was transformed, as if the hands of time had turned backwards, and Don, young once again, would enter, pail in hand. Standing in the center of the room, I could imagine it ready for work, complete with a stainless-steel sink and draining tables. The fridge would be in that corner, its glass display doors enticing with bottles of milk and neat rows of cheese. Against the other wall, tall racks would hold stacks of cheese molds. And if the white walls were not allowed to hold photos, at least they would bear our license as a grade-A dairy!

A certified milk room was a work of love and patience, and I laugh as I remember Don's stories. A practical man, Don knew the demands of farming, but he also knew he had to please the inspectors. When they gave him a list of improvements, he would simply pick one.

In the early years of his marriage, the milk inspector had been a particularly stern man, and Don, unable to resist some gentle fun, had posted a poem he'd written on the wall.

To the Milk Inspector for His Consideration

From early in the morning
till late at night we toil,
for if we feed our cows
we must build up the soil.

We work all kinds of weather,
in snow and wind and rain,
hoping when our check gets here
'twill buy groceries and grain.

We are wondering if our place
will pass the test or not.
We're doing just the best we can
on seven cents a quart.

The inspection had proceeded without much comment until finally, the inspector was getting ready to leave.

"Did you read my poem?" Don asked, eyes twinkling, as the inspector bent to slip off his boots.

Pulling a little more insistently at an apparently stubborn boot, the inspector finally replied, "I think you overdid it on the seven cents."

Now Brandon was helping us restore the dairy. It would be up to us to make it work, in snow and wind and rain—and current market conditions! We had a long way to go before we would be commercial, but at least our steps were now as concrete as the birthday we would soon be celebrating.

Reminded of the present, I check my watch. Joe Heaney, a local builder, would be arriving any minute, and I would need to show him around the barn.

A skilled timber framer, Joe specialized in barn restoration, and we had asked him to evaluate the structural soundness of our barn. We would eventually need to build a separate milking parlor for milking the does, and I was unsure whether the existing floor could bear the added weight.

We had first met Joe when he was working on my parents' sagging old barn, stripping it down to its beams and then building it back up, straight and clean, its youthful beauty restored. Whereas my parents had renovated their entire barn, our aims—like our budget—were much more modest. We needed only to repair the addition at the back, a long, low-ceilinged room that had been built in the 1920s, when function trumped form. Appraising the floor beams, above and below, Joe is all business, evaluating integrity without reference to aesthetics.

Still, the bulk of the barn beckons mysteriously from the small doorway, so I lead him into the main floor.

"Oh, it's timber-framed," he says in sudden delight as we turn the corner and the tall beams of the hayloft rise above us. He pauses, a craftsman admiring the skill of another generation, and we look up in shared appreciation of its beauty.

Slowly we wander the length of the barn, like tourists in a cathedral, while I tell him a little of the farm's history.

Joe points out some tall posts, their tops wider than their base. "Those are gunstock beams," he says. "They stopped doing that around 1829."

Surprised, I frown. "But Julia and Ephraim didn't start building our house until 1830," I tell him.

He grins, confident in both craft and history.

"Yes," he replies, "they often built the barn before the house. Look," he continues, directing my eye now to a long crossbeam, "you can tell that is hand-hewn by the adze marks."

Looking up, I see for the first time the soft sculpting of the beam, each swing of the adze visible, and behind it the sweat and skill of another generation. As Joe turns, piecing together the story of the barn, I reach out to touch the post, the past suddenly alive under my hand.

By the time I wave Joe off, I am in a happy daze of history, but the sight of Brandon rounding the corner clears away the fog. He looks less than pleased, and I can tell the butchering was not as easy as he had been promised. However, before I can ask, Keiran spies me and runs outside, desperate to join the action. Brandon looks at him in amazement, and I grin at the two of them in amused compassion. This is Keiran's world, for better or worse, and he knows its rules.

"I want to hear about it later," I tell Brandon, to which he shivers, replying, "Yuck."

Taking Keiran's hand—now a privilege, not a necessity—I escort my small farmer across the lawn. However, maternal affection is forgotten as he spies the men gathered around the birch trees.

"Daddy," he cries, running across the lawn, and the men turn, parting to reveal the hanging goat, naked without its skin.

An experienced team, they work quickly now, and Anil, a good teacher, stands aside while Alex cuts the meat.

While Keiran admires Alex's handiwork, I tell Anil about Joe's comments. Finally, this month, it felt like the farm was growing again, its future as hopeful as Keiran's. We grin at each other, glad for the celebration, farm and family twining around each other. Leaving the birthday boy absorbed in dinner preparations, I head back inside, to secret birthday tasks.

First there is a tractor cake to attend to, and the question of whether to color the frosting John Deere green or Kubota orange. Luckily, I have plenty of help from Keiran's aunties and cousins. While I fuss with the finer points of tractor decoration, they cut out paper hats, decorating them with moose horns and bullfrog tongues, the magical creatures which currently populate Keiran's imagination. Their designs—more whimsical than realistic—keep us all laughing until we hear Keiran returning and hide them away.

Flushed with excitement, Keiran is reluctant to nap. However, finally convinced, he sleeps soundly, leaving me free to start dinner. Like all good meals, this one is planned around local harvests, so I head out to the garden to survey our options. Although the full potato harvest will not be for another month, we can safely harvest a few of the small "new" potatoes without damage to the plants.

Kneeling, I show Keiran's cousins how to "rob" the potatoes. Feeling around carefully in the dirt, I select a few good-size tubers to pull. When the potatoes pop out of the ground, their smooth skins shining like buried treasure, the girls need no further encouragement. They kneel in the dirt beside me, delighted to discover not only yellow but red and blue potatoes, like unexpected Easter eggs in their hands. When our baskets are full, we harvest some fresh herbs, strewing them on top of the potatoes like meadow flowers.

While I dice the potatoes, sprinkling them with minced herbs, Alex and Anil tend to the goat. We often curry goat meat, but this was a very young animal, so we have decided to roast a whole leg and some ribs for good measure. We let Alex, our grilling king in residence, take charge of the meat. A master of spices, he decides to showcase the taste of the fresh tender meat by roasting it unadorned.

ALEX'S ROAST LEG OF GOAT

Choose a whole leg of a young kid goat. Remove as much of the whitish outer membrane as possible to lessen the "goaty" taste. Rub with olive oil, then sprinkle with salt and pepper and blacken on a hot grill. Wrap in foil and slow cook on the coals until meat reaches 145 degrees. Let rest for ten minutes before slicing thinly and serving.

Meanwhile, guests arrive, bearing bounty from their own gardens. Our friend Debbi brings a salad of purple carrots and feta, and Mom slips in her green beans, steamed just enough to brighten their color.

Bottles of Alex's homemade beer appear in unsuspecting hands, and guests swirl between kitchen and grill, laughter weaving them together.

Dinner officially begins when Don and Shirley arrive, back from the funeral of a beloved teacher. Still, it is Shirley, and sadness slides into joy, as she comments, "It's not bad going from a funeral to the birthday of a two-year-old." We all laugh, with compassion and awareness, and head in to the meal. With so many of us, we sit elbow to elbow, with room only for stories.

The meal—simple in many ways—is yet good enough to quiet us momentarily. The potatoes, diced and roasted, are rich, as if it's the first time you ever really *tasted* a potato, full of life and complexity. The goat, sliced into slivers or gnawed off the bone, needs no adornment; a bowl of barbecue sauce sits unused on the table. Full of color and flavor, the vegetables break juicy on our tongue with all the sweet succulence of summer.

Perhaps it is the food, or perhaps it is Alex's beer, but eventually my father pushes back from the table, overcome. Curious, we turn quiet, and he looks around at our encircling eyes and grins.

"I've eaten more delicious meals here!" he declares, and, laughing, we all cheer. For we know the meal is not just food—it is the connection to earth and sky, plant and animal. A life has been taken, work has been shared, and now we have come together. This is life, the pumpkin vines that bind us together as family.

It is also a two-year-old's party, and, with less to ponder, the demand for dessert is soon upon us. Luckily, the adorned tractor cake, resplendent in orange, is met with approval, although we are not given long to admire before it is time to taste. In attendance as bullfrogs and bull moose, the need for manners is less, and chocolate disappears greedily, no crumb wasted.

Amidst the chaos of a happy party, I overhear my father saying to Don, "You must have been to many birthdays here." Sliding between guests, the words sink in slowly, blossoming. Here Don would have celebrated his own childhood birthdays, surrounded by parents and grandparents . . .

NOTES

1. Alex in Maine, Anil in Trinidad, and Albert El-Hage in Lebanon.
2. Brandon Klein, my first cousin once removed.

1939

DON HEWETT

SNOW IS piled high along the edges of the road, and sleigh bells jingle in the distance. A team of horses appears around the corner, their breath steaming in the cold, but instead of the expected sleigh, they pull a car, its motor stubbornly quiet.

Seventeen-year-old Don Hewett sits on the hood, reins in hand, while his brother Lloyd, twenty, steers the car. The horses pull with goodwill, gaining speed, until the car's engine finally roars into life. With a shout, Don jumps down, unhitching the horses. Lloyd would have to return them to the barn; Don still had to drive the twenty miles to Augusta before the school bells rang.

In his senior year at Cony High School, Don arrived late more often than he—or his teachers—would have liked. Every morning he tried to hurry through chores, but cows did not like to be rushed, and he was frequently delayed. Frowning, the class advisor reminded him that *she* also lived twenty miles away, but *she* managed to be on time. Sitting through yet another detention, Don was tempted to ask her how many cows *she* had to milk before school.

Despite his tardiness, Don was, and always had been, a good student. Neither his mother nor the young teachers who boarded with them had ever allowed farm work to be an excuse for missing school. Don, in fact, quite liked school, and, as an elementary student, had willingly made the daily walk to the South Somerville School, the one-room schoolhouse that lay a mile down the road. In his final year, his diligence was rewarded, for he earned the highest rank in the school union.

Now, he was almost through high school, and he faced a tough decision: His chemistry teacher was urging him to go to college, but his father had recently been diagnosed with multiple sclerosis by a doctor in Boston. Although they didn't make much money, Don knew his father loved farm life and would struggle to keep it going despite his declining health. As for Don, he loved both his father and the farm—it was, after all, his inheritance from five generations. So at eighteen years old, Don accepted a partnership in his father's dairy farm, assuming he'd "just go along as the generations before had."

In fact, unlike other generations, Don did not plan to make any radical alterations to his father's operation. In the past decade, Lloyd had shifted his production to accommodate changes in the market, ensuring the farm's continued profitability. For many years, only the cream had commercial value, while the skimmed milk was fed to pigs and calves. However, the demand for fresh milk had steadily increased during the 1930s,[1] and Lloyd had gradually shifted entirely to milk production. In 1933, when the narrow gauge railway was discontinued, Lloyd, like many other dairy farmers,[2] had arranged for a truck to pick up his milk. Now, instead of the six-mile trek to Cooper's Mills, Don only had to jog the horses to the end of the road, where he left the milk cans on a platform.

Despite such changes, the daily routine of farming was the same— had been the same since Don had started milking at the age of seven. Milking was the framework of his day, his greeting to the dawn and his farewell to the night. Rising at five a.m., he dressed and went straight to the barn, scooping the grain as quickly as he could to quiet the hungry cows. The barn, warmed by the cows' bodies, was comfortable even in winter, and the lanterns which hung from the crossbeams kept the darkness at bay. While the cows ate, he shoveled out the pens and spread fresh sawdust, filling the air with the sweet scent of pulverized wood. Only then, when the pens were clean, did he start milking.

He milked by hand, moving his stool down the line of cows. His hands were accustomed to the rhythm, and the milk sprang forth in rich, white jets, foaming as it filled the pail. When no more milk could be coaxed out, he strained it into the tall cans they used for storage. Full cans were kept in an ice bath, a concrete tank ingeniously built into the floor of the barn, making it easy to pull the heavy cans out.

After milking there was hay to feed, the sweet, dried stalks pitched into each crib, the barn slowly filling with the quiet grinding of stems and leaves. Fresh water was pumped by hand from dug wells, insulated from freezing temperatures by the residual heat of the earth. Not until eight or nine did he remember his own breakfast and head back home, suddenly in a hurry, leaving the milking equipment to clean up afterwards.

In the summer the cows were out on pasture and came in only to be milked, waiting at the fence like children anxious for recess. With no barn to clean, and less need for hay and grain, morning chores went more quickly. Breakfast came earlier, but not in exchange for leisure, for now it was the growing season, and all of life burst forth, urgently demanding attention.

Haying was such a large part of life that his mother often said there were only two seasons on the farm: "haying and cutting wood." From late June through September, days were spent in the field, mowing, raking, and tedding the hay. The grass had to be carefully tended as it dried to prepare it for its long winter storage. Wet hay would rot, and the heat of decomposition could start a catastrophic barn fire.

Once the grass was cut, everyone watched the sky, balancing an extra hour of drying against the possibility of rain. When it was time to move, all hands assembled to get the hay safely from field to barn. The loose hay was pitched by hand into huge piles on the wagon. Deceptively simple, there was actually an art to building a load, as the loose hay could easily snarl, making it impossible to gather or separate. As the men pitched it in, children would tread it down until the load rose high in the air. When it could hold no more, the wagon, only its wheels visible under its shaggy mane of hay, was carefully driven back to the barn.

To get the hay up to the loft, a pulley was rigged on a high beam. A fork on one end was plunged deep into the hay, while the other end was attached to the horses. When the horses were led out of the barn, the loaded fork was propelled up to the loft where the hay was packed into huge, fragrant piles. Back and forth the horses went, in and out, in and out, sending the hay up to the loft one forkful at a time.

As a boy, Don had kept an eye on the bottom pulley, clearing away any loose hay before it could jam. More eager than cautious, he had caught his hand under the pulley. Luckily, his loud screams kept him from losing more than a finger; his father immediately stopped the horses and his mother, picking raspberries a half-mile away, came running to his aid. Since then, nine fingers had done the work of ten without complaint or rancor.

Although there was lots of work, there was often an excuse for fun. When a farmer harvested his feed corn, he would throw a husking party, and the neighbors would gather to help. Young men would husk energetically, stripping the ears with enthusiasm, for if they found a red ear of corn, they were allowed to kiss the girl of their choice. Thinking only of present delights, they did not know they were following ancient traditions, for the red ear ritual was originally a Native American custom.[3] Regardless of origin, the ensuing frolic shared the same pleasures and perils, for the intended recipient was not always well pleased to be chosen.

Although social activities were sporadic, the land itself provided year-round entertainment. The small brook was yet large enough to provide fishing and rafting in the summer and skating in the winter. One year Don and Lloyd strapped old skates on two-by-fours and made an iceboat. Although the sail could not compensate for the weight of the wood, they pushed it with goodwill, jumping on when it gathered momentum. The hills offered endless sledding on slopes of all degrees, from the novice to the daredevil.

So the years had gone by, and if their passing was noted, it was mainly by the arrival, each year, of his grandmother Edith's lemon pie, made especially for Don on his birthday, and still his favorite:

Grandma Edith's Lemon Pie

Moisten a heaping teaspoon of cornstarch with a little cold water, then add a cupful of boiling water, stir over the fire until it boils and cooks the starch, say 2 or 3 minutes. Add a teaspoonful of butter and a cupful of sugar. Take off the fire and when slightly cooled, add an egg, well beaten, and the grated rind and juice of one lemon. If baking with one crust, leave out the white of the egg for frosting.

For the frosting, beat the white of the egg until very stiff, then add 3 heaping tablespoons of sugar. Flavor with vanilla, and beat stiff. When the pie is baked, which is quickly done, add the frosting and return to the oven until frosting is browned.

Now, however, seventeen years had passed—seventeen lemon pies, Don thought with a grin—and he was no longer a boy but a farmer, and soon, a business partner. Although he knew he would have a lot more responsibilities in the years ahead, he assumed things on the farm would continue much as they had.

Life, however, had other plans; much was soon to change, both at home and in the broader world.

One year later, in the spring of 1940, his grandmother Edith passed away, a month before Don's eighteenth birthday. For the first time, his lemon pie, lovingly made by his mother, was more sour than sweet in his mouth. Edith's absence was felt keenly by all, and they held more tightly to each other in their grief, her love binding them together.

Unable to bear the silence of his house, Don's grandfather, William, moved in with them, but memory followed Will, and every day he returned to light the woodstove, warming the empty house. Don and Lloyd, busy cutting firewood, would look up and see the chimney smoking, devouring their hard-earned harvest.

"There goes the factory," Lloyd would mutter, in mock indignation.

Firewood, however, was soon to be the least of their concerns. On December 7, 1941, the United States entered into World War II, and the military begin drafting young men into service. As a farmer, Don was exempt from the war, his agricultural production deemed more important to national security than his presence at the front. Lloyd, however, was a carpenter, and in 1943, after a hurried wedding to Marjorie Clark, he was sent to New Guinea.

Now, it was Don at home—Don and his parents and the cows. Although he enjoyed working the land with his father, it was at times hard to be home when all of his friends were serving. Almost every eligible young man—and, for the first time, some women—from Somerville had enlisted,[4] and social gatherings were quiet, without the exuberance of youth. More than ever, Don's parents relied on him, strengthened by his gentle commitment to them and his skillful management of the farm.

Together, they kept a herd of forty-five Holstein cows, with about twenty-five milking at any one time. As cows filled up the barn, they abandoned the poultry business to make room for sawdust and shavings. Although wartime production had boosted the economy, effectively ending the Great Depression, Don was not convinced by the new flush of wealth. He had seen his parents survive the Great Depression on credit, and he vowed never to buy what he could not afford.

Frugal and committed, he farmed carefully, learning all that he could. When his father Lloyd had begun farming, he had relied on the steady strength of oxen to break new ground. Oxen, however, required two men to plow—one man to drive the animals, and one to guide the plow. Don, increasingly on his own, turned more and more to horses, as he could drive them alone, guiding them with long reins over their necks.

More than technical skill, working with horses required patience to establish mutual respect with the powerful and often headstrong animals. This was a long-term relationship, often lasting for twenty years or more, and it was important to get off to a good start. Don, ever patient and respectful, understood the needs of his fellow creatures, and softened his voice and gentled his hand to earn their trust.

One haying season, in need of a third horse, Don approached the local "horse jockey," a dealer who brought in workhorses from the Midwest. A few days later, the dealer arrived with a young horse shod only on its front hooves. Dubious, Don eyed the horse, inquiring if it was hard to shoe. The dealer assured Don that he just hadn't gotten to it yet, and bent to pick up a hind foot. With one swift shove, the horse sent the man tumbling backwards. Trying to keep a straight face, Don mumbled something about not being interested. The dealer, however, was more eager than ever for a sale, and quickly backed away, calling, "I'll just leave him a few days . . ."

Watching the horse over the stable door, Don wondered what to do. The horse was, in fact, a nice-looking animal, its rich, black coat a perfect match to his other two horses. Seeking advice, he visited a local blacksmith, who suggested that he harness the new horse to an experienced horse, then work them hard on soft ground. Only when the horse was tired should Don approach it, patting it and slowly working his way down to its feet.

Armed with such sound advice, Don decided to keep the horse, and so Duke joined the farm. With calm and consistent handling, Duke became a solid member of the team; in fact, he liked to work, and protested if he was left alone in the barn. Now that Don could pick up all four hooves, he just needed shoes.

Given the heavy work they did, workhorses needed new shoes every two to three months, and it was often hard to get a blacksmith. However, since they had a forge at the farm, Don, undaunted, decided to try it himself. While he may have lacked training, he had plenty of opportunities to perfect his technique, and from then on Don shod his own horses, including the special sharpened winter shoes.

Winter was the best time to harvest wood, but forest trails were usually slick with ice. To pull out heavy loads, the horses needed spiked shoes to get a grip on the slippery trails. If the snow was too deep, Don would walk ahead, breaking a trail. He appreciated the horses' willing cooperation, and would look for a sheltered spot to tie them. Blanketed and with bags of hay, they waited patiently while he worked.

In the summer they spent many hours plowing the fields, each year reseeding a new piece. This was tedious work for man and horse, as they had to go slowly, guiding the plow through the rocky soil. Mostly Don could just wiggle the plow through a rough spot, but large rocks required them to stop and lift the plow over.

Working together over the years, man and horses came to rely on each other, appreciating the little quirks that might otherwise be maddening. More than draft power alone, these were individuals, and they earned their place in the history of the farm. So Barney, a notoriously lazy horse, was remembered with affectionate despair. Whereas most horses would immediately jump up if they fell, Barney would lie there contentedly, as if glad for the rest.

Bound to the farm by the love of his family, Don also found deep satisfaction in his work. Gently easing the load off his father's shoulders, he gradually took on more responsibilities. Challenging as the war years were, they nonetheless served him well, and by the time the war ended in 1945, Don was an established farmer.

Satisfied perhaps that his vision of a dairy farm was in competent hands, William Hewett passed on in January 1946. He had chosen wisely at a time when Maine agriculture was in transition, and had lived to see his farm support both his son and grandson. Never one to shirk a job, he had finally taken his rest, and the farm was quieter without his powerful energy.

Thankfully, Lloyd came home from the war soon afterwards, bringing life back to the empty house. Though neither Lloyd nor Marge was fond of farming, they valued family ties and wanted to raise their children surrounded by the noisy chaos of cousins.

While Marge's belly swelled with new life, the farm also trembled with great expectations, for they were soon to have electricity! Under Roosevelt's Rural Electrification Administration,[5] Somerville was waiting to be connected to the electrical grid. With great anticipation, Don watched the poles going up, slowly advancing along the road. When they finally reached the farm, he wasted no time in putting his connection to use. In house and barn, lanterns were put away forever as electric lights replaced kerosene.

By far the greatest advantage, however, was for the farm. Their first priority was to have a new well drilled, with an electric pump. Water now flowed into the barn at the twist of a tap, eliminating many hours of pumping and hauling heavy buckets. Their next major investment was a refrigerated bulk tank to quickly cool the milk. Now they no longer needed ice, freeing them from another tedious daily chore. Best of all, the electricity cost no more than the ice had! Since they had a bulk tank, the milk truck drove right up to the farm, collecting the milk through its long hose. From a farmer's perspective, electrification was indeed the "greatest engineering achievement of the twentieth century."[6]

While Don was guiding his farm through the rapid changes of modernization, his brother Lloyd was building a family. Lloyd's first son, Denis, was born in 1947, followed by his first daughter, Jean, in 1949. Tragically, Denis was lost to cancer, and the family huddled close with the pain of losing one so young. A farm was surrounded by life and death, but it also had seasons, and the betrayal of natural rhythms felt all the more senseless.

Surrounded by his brother's growing family, Don too had a wife in mind. At twenty-eight years old, he was not only an established dairy farmer, but also first selectman of Somerville, and he frequently had to consult with Charles Brown, the town treasurer and tax collector. Without a town office, meetings were held at home, and luckily for Don, Charles shared a home with an attractive young niece, Shirley Brown.

Being at heart a country girl, Shirley had refused her brother's urging to attend school in Boston. In partial concession, she had agreed to business school in Augusta, where she boarded at the Girls' Club, guarded by a vigilant house mother. Despite her recent move to town, Don knew that her father was a farmer, and that she, in fact, preferred country life.

Still, she was only nineteen years old—nine years his junior—and he was a little apprehensive about approaching her. However, he knew he could not wait; he was not the only one to notice the pretty young woman!

Summoning his courage, he invited her to the movies, only to be refused; Shirley had just washed her hair, and it needed time to set. Suspecting he was being put off, Don nevertheless persisted, and they made another date. This time, the results were worse: They confused their meeting time, so that each waited—in vain—for the other.

Amazingly, they agreed to try again, and finally Don escorted young Shirley Brown to the movies. It was, in fact, the second time Shirley had been asked to that particular movie, but, more interested in Don than the film, she kept this fact to herself. The movie itself was soon forgotten, but Shirley's fancy was forever taken by the handsome young farmer.

Shirley enjoyed country life, and it was not long before she followed Don home to the farm. Romance or no romance, the cows still had to be milked, and so she went with him, helping him as he worked his way down the line of animals. The rhythm of farm life was familiar to her, and she had mourned its loss as a child. Now, finally, she felt at home again, comfortable with this gentle young farmer. They worked together naturally, laughing, and when he proposed to her in the barn, she sealed the bargain with a kiss.

On October 13, 1951, Don and Shirley were married at the South Somerville Baptist Church, only a mile down the road from his farm. After a honeymoon in Niagara Falls, the newlyweds moved back to the farm—and in with Don's parents. Happy to have the young couple staying on the farm, Lloyd and Jane had moved upstairs, leaving Shirley and Don the first floor.

Finally at home on her own farm, Shirley still had one big challenge—the kitchen. As a new wife with a hardworking farmer to feed, Shirley was at a loss; no one had ever taught her to cook. When her first batch of biscuits was refused by the family dog, she went upstairs in search of her mother-in-law. Jennie welcomed her new daughter with a smile, and Shirley stood at her elbow while she mixed and delicately shaped the dough.

Maine's new secret ingredient, Bakewell Cream, promised to make biscuits lighter and higher than ever before. Developed during the war when baking powder and cream of tartar were scarce, it used an alternative leavening agent that delighted the hand of Maine cooks and the palate of Maine diners.[7] Perhaps it was the Bakewell Cream, or the enfolding love of a mother, but Shirley's biscuits were never refused again.

SHIRLEY HEWETT'S BISCUITS

2 cups flour
2 tsp Bakewell Cream
1 tsp baking soda
½ tsp salt
¼ cup shortening
¾ cup cold milk

Mix together the flour, cream, soda, and salt. Melt the shortening and stir in along with the cold milk. Gently pat dough out on a floured board and cut into squares. Bake at 475 degrees for 5 minutes, then turn off oven and leave in for 5 to 10 more minutes, until golden brown.

NOTES

1. Day, *Farming in Maine*, p. 179.

2. Russell, *A Long, Deep Furrow*, p. 301.

3. Stavely and Fitzgerald, *America's Founding Food*, p. 43.

4. Allard, French, Cranmer, and Milakovsky, *Then & Now: Patricktown/ Somerville. Volume Two: History*, p. 12.

5. http://www.greatachievements.org/.

6. Ibid., as declared by the National Academy of Engineering.

7. http://www.newenglandcupboard.com/about-us.php.

August 2010

Barn

THE FIRST week of August, and Anil is ill. One night, our guests departing, he looks at me with bleary eyes, rubbing his temples. My arms full with Sarita, I press my lips against his forehead, and his face flushes hot against mine. At night his whole body trembles with fever, and he asks, in the darkness, "What would you do without me?" Teasing, I reassure him that we have life insurance, but he ignores my joke. "Would the kids remember me?" he asks, and I feel the sudden gap of death and too familiar absence.

For a week he sleeps constantly, hardly eating, rising only to drink water. We track the swift ascent of his fever and the gradual descent, then wait, in what seems an endless drag of days, for his energy to return. Alone with the kids night and day, I struggle with my own fatigue, fighting to stay awake, and positive. At times I feel hopeless, becalmed, forgetting what it feels like to laugh, to hope, to plan, to move.

The children also fight small fevers, and I help them as best I can. Stripped down to his diaper, Keiran sweats all day, his damp hair plastered to his head. Easily frustrated, he cries as his new tractor breaks. Sarita sleeps and sleeps, naptime turning into nighttime, drugged by fever. Beset by microscopic invaders, the children's small bodies are fierce battlegrounds, and life, so recently joined, seems a fragile thread.

Exhausted, I scarcely look outside, grateful that the goats have ample pasture. Mercifully, the animals are largely self-sufficient in the summer, and the farm demands little of its ailing caretakers. In fact, it is the farm that offers a ray of hope, penetrating our collective delirium.

Reluctantly answering the phone one evening, I find myself reminded of larger dreams, of health and growth. Joe's warm voice floods across the phone lines, filling the dimly lit kitchen with the solid hope of reality. He has put a letter in the mail, with a proposal to repair not only the floor, but to frame up the walls of our milking parlor.

A milking parlor!

With the milk room now cleaned and painted, our license is suddenly within reach. In between visiting sickbeds, I study our finances, trying to find the balance between moving forward and leaping off a cliff. During the day I make phone calls, evaluating materials, balancing cost with durability. At night my parents call to check on us, mixing medical advice with building recommendations.

One evening, juggling both children in the bathtub, I hear Anil's footsteps in the kitchen and the soft ping of the computer as he checks e-mail. I turn in surprise, delighted to see him upright and smiling.

"Your parents want to help with the barn," he says, and I stare at him blankly, aware only of relief. "Go check e-mail," he says, taking the kids' towels out of my hand. As he bends to sit by the bathtub, solid and engaged in life, I feel time once again moving forward, the world suddenly whole.

Curious now, I head to the computer, pulling up my parents' message. Although they doubt the economic viability of a small farm, they know we will never make any money if we do not have a licensed milk room. To that end, they are willing to pay a large portion of the repair costs, as long as we get it done soon and properly.

I look up, trying to focus on reality, my emotions in free fall, sliding through surprise—disbelief—delight—into humble gratitude. Their message is like a beacon from the future, beckoning from a place of health and possibility. With their help, our dreams are suddenly closer, the farm coming back to life, woven with the love and support of family: Pumpkin Vine Family Farm indeed!

Toy hammer in hand, Keiran waits impatiently for the barn work to begin. Unfortunately, we had scheduled a doctor's appointment for the first morning of work, and I am buckling the kids into the car as Joe arrives. Seeing the truck, Keiran strains against his straps, protesting, desperate to follow Joe into the barn. However, mindful of time, I back the car out of the garage, ignoring his pleas. But his wails are not in vain. Penetrating metal and glass, they reach Joe, who takes pity and comes over to say hello. Suddenly quiet, Keiran looks at Joe in awe, but his irrepressible smile returns.

By the time we return home, Keiran is asleep in his car seat, but he rises to consciousness with a destination in mind.

"Keiran go in the barn?" he implores, and this time we humor him, for we are all eager to see how the work has progressed.

Keiran, desperate to get inside, pushes in front of us, then stops, stunned, as the door swings wide. The majority of the floorboards have been pulled up, leaving a gaping hole in the middle of the room. Intrigued to see the barn's inner structure, Anil and I walk around the edge, pointing out rotten beams and patched joints. Keiran scrambles after us, peering through the exposed beams to the dirt beneath.

Discussing the layout of the new milking parlor, I am only half aware of Keiran, his usual monologue pitched high with shock. Finally, however, his distress penetrates my consciousness, and I turn to listen.

"Keiran's barn broken," he repeats over and over. "Keiran sad, Keiran's barn broken down."

Understanding his confusion, we explain that the crossbeams must be repaired before a new floor can be put in place. He listens without further comment, trusting us, but he looks suspiciously at the suddenly unfamiliar barn.

The next morning, Keiran watches through his bedroom window as Joe and Eric unload their tools. While I strap Sarita into a front pack, he makes his own preparations, running between his tool bench and the window, checking his tools against theirs. Finally settling on his hammer and saw, he is ready for work, but once in the barn he falls quiet, listening intently to the men's quick banter.

Well-read and well-rounded, Joe and Eric are both storytellers, and their conversation spans many topics besides the job at hand. When Joe eventually brings the talk back to the barn, Eric brings over an old beam, turning it so we can see the rot underneath. Although reluctant to speak, Keiran is quick with his hammer, banging the board as Eric holds it out for our examination. Laughing, Joe cautions Eric: "Don't let him do that too long, or you'll have to pay him!"

On the way home, Keiran pulls me in a wide detour to the trailer that serves as their toolshed. Carefully surveying the tools, he places his hammer next to their large mauls, aligning its small plastic head with their heavy iron ones. I watch quietly, letting him claim a place in the action, knowing the men will not mind.

The next day I venture out alone while the children nap, and Joe greets me with a laugh.

"Did Keiran tell you what he did?" he asks, and I feign ignorance, letting them describe their discovery, delight evident in their voices. They are flattered by his interest, and before I leave, Eric hands me a pencil to give to Keiran. Squared and red, it is unmistakably a carpenter's pencil, and Keiran claims it with delight when he awakens, proud to be a recognized part of the crew.

Day after day, the barn is transformed, renewed, her old bones exposed and repaired. The new flooring goes in quickly, accompanied by the hum of the compressor and the rapid fire of the pneumatic hammer. As the hole is covered, the new wood, sturdy and golden with youth, makes the room shine, and we dance on it in the evenings in a private celebration of renewal. Immensely relieved to have his barn restored, Keiran hops the length of the floor, pleased by his rhythmic thumping. Watching his delight, I wonder what Don will think of the transformation.

That weekend, I find Don by his toolshed, changing the spark plugs on the old John Deere. He straightens when I walk up, glad to chat. He knew we were having work done on the barn, and he had seen the piles of lumber growing and shifting, new wood going in, old wood coming out. With his usual thoughtful courtesy, he had declined to visit in the thick of construction, but today he accepts gladly.

He knows I love to hear the farm's history, and I match my pace to his while he points out the features of the past, the dusty clutter less real than the breath of memory. Those walls had been solid then, and the hay went up there. There he had lost his finger as a young boy, and those numbers were for his daughter Sylvie, so she knew how much grain to feed each cow.

The new section is in the very back, and, with a lifetime of experience, he ducks his head under a low—and mercilessly hard—beam that separates the old barn from the new. The room is open, undivided, and the floor shines in the sunlight. Don looks around quietly, his hands still at his sides, and I hold my breath, wondering if I have made a mistake.

Looking at the new floor, I had seen love and hope, but I had not considered all that we had removed. For all the years of Don's life, from young boy to working father, this had been a dairy barn, and under its shelter he had built up his herd and his family. Here the cows had been tied up, awaiting his twice-daily milking, and as he worked his way down the stalls, he had known continuity as well as change. Here he had proposed to his wife, and here he had helped his young daughter find meaning and joy.

The individual stalls had been unnecessary for our purposes, so we had asked Joe to tear them down when he took up the floor. Now, looking at the empty room, I realized it was sturdy but bare, a clean slate awaiting a new hand. Hopeful life, yes, but not Don's life, and his years of work suddenly, irrevocably, existed in memory alone.

As I waver nervously, he looks at me, smiling his calm smile, and I breathe out, relieved if rueful. Emboldened, I ask if he wants to see the milk room, now fully restored in its coat of white paint. Agreeable as ever, he follows me through the door, then stops and turns in evident delight.

"It looks good," he says, surprised by its familiarity, for we have changed little, only repaired the cracks. His bulk tank had stood in here, and the marks of its legs are still evident on the floor. Returned to familiar ground, he slides back into stories as we head out.

Forever a curious farmer, he peers into the pigpen as we pass by. He stops, admiring, for Rhodora has grown large, and her red coat gleams with health.

"We named her Rhodora," I tell him, "in honor of the wild plants we found in the back field."[1]

"Rhodora," Don says, standing suddenly straight as a schoolboy and clearing his throat:

Rhodora! if the sages ask thee why
This charm is wasted on the earth and sky,
Tell them, dear, that if eyes were made for seeing,
Then Beauty is its own excuse for being.[2]

Stopping, he laughs, sheepishly proud.

"We had to learn that in school," he explains, "but I can't remember the rest."

Openmouthed, I stare, amazed by his sudden transformation, the familiar stoop of his shoulders replaced by the stretching reach of a young sapling. Slightly dizzy, I look at him and try to focus.

Standing in the barn, he is solid and calm, a tree deeply rooted, and I feel again the guest, restless as the flitting swallows.

Surprised in turn by my silence, he looks at me, his eyes twinkling, at once young and old. Together we laugh now, joined by the surprising beauty of our large red pig, anchoring our present in his past.

NOTES

1. Rhodora is a wild member of the rhododendron family.
2. From the poem "The Rhodora," by Ralph Waldo Emerson (see Appendix II for full text).

1952

DON AND SHIRLEY HEWETT

SUMMERTIME, and the road is surrounded by waving fields of grass, waiting for the passage of the mowing machine. It is still early, but farmers should be at work, for hay needs a full day to dry. However, there is a new sound on the road, a sputtering rumble, coming from the barn. The sun, soft and golden, blinks in surprise as the farmer emerges; he drives not a team of horses but a tall, sputtering machine, a mower following obediently behind. Effortlessly, the tractor's tall wheels roll down the road, leaving a long, seamless trail in the dirt. With a magician's wave, Don turns it into the field, heading with purpose into the tall grass.

Don had bought his first tractor that spring, a secondhand Model B John Deere, its tall, narrow frame affording him a commanding view of his fields. He was glad to turn over the haying to the tractor, for mowing was hard work for the horses, especially on a hot day. Flies would buzz incessantly around their eyes and ears, and the harnessed horses could only stamp and twitch in unrelieved agony. Now, with the tractor, he need not worry about the horses, and he could accomplish so much more.

The gas-powered engine, harvesting the power of carbon, forever freed farmers from the limits of animal endurance. Oil and coal, slowly accumulated, were now rapidly released, the stored energy of the earth transformed into the rapid pulses of mechanized agriculture. Engines, measured in terms of "horsepower," increased in size so quickly that actual horse power was soon considered a hobbyist's choice.

The John Deere "General Purpose" tractors, built during the 1920s and 1930s, had a pulling capacity of six horses; tireless, they boasted a "daily work output" of eight or ten horses. Brochures for the Model A claimed that "it puts into the hands of one man the working capacity of three to six men ..."

The Model B tractor, two-thirds the size of the A, was purposefully designed for small, diversified farms, and was "ready to prepare seed beds, plant and cultivate row crops, handle your haying operations, operate your harvesting equipment, cut ensilage, grind feed ... handle any farm job within its power range."[1]

The tractor was, from the first, a lifesaver for Don. With a new wife and a sick father, the ability to get more done—as much as three or four men!—allowed him to juggle the responsibilities of family and farm. For now there was a young wife waiting when he came in to breakfast, offering the labor of her hands with pride.

After the sweetness of a meal together, there was a moment of parting, where before there had just been work. As he sat down to slide on his work boots, Shirley would often climb onto his lap, laughing and pleading with him not to leave. But Mother Nature moved with her own urgency, and the changing seasons demanded constant attention, for a week too late could mean another year's wait. And so Don rose and went out, with a parting kiss to sweeten the work ahead.

In spring, with green flushing the pasture and cows restless in the barn, he tended first to the fence line. During May he traced the perimeter of his pastures, checking for trees fallen across wires or posts thrown loose by frost. He followed the barbed wire as it plunged into the woods, enclosing a shadowy world of trees and moss, suitable for the yearling stock. Too young to be milked, the heifers were free to roam distant pastures, drinking from springs and bogs.

In late May and early June, Don plowed and reseeded part of the pasture, ensuring that all the fields were reseeded every seven or eight years. With the walking plow, this had been an arduous task, but Don hoped the tractor would make quick work of it.

However, even advanced technology had to contend with nature. When Don set the tractor to the task, the rocky Maine soil stymied the plow, forcing him to climb down to clear away boulders. When the morning was over, he had gained little; horses could have covered the ground in the same amount of time.

When the fields dried out in June, he started spreading manure, transforming the steaming piles of waste into rich renewal. As a boy, he had pitched manure out of the wagon by hand, the benefit obscured by the difficult, noisome task. Now, his tractor pulled a mechanized spreader, casting the manure in a wide swath and making short work of the job.

As June turned into July, Don settled into haying. The tractor circled steadily around the field, never tiring, pulling first mower, then tedder, then rake. Finally the baler arrived like a hungry factory, transforming the loose grass into tightly bound rectangles. With bales there was also an art to loading the wagon, weaving them in a tight crisscross to resist the pull of gravity. As the wagon trundled across the rough ground, the load trembled, as precarious as a small child's tower of blocks, and the stacker's reputation was earned or lost based on skill and ability.

At the barn, the pulley was replaced by a conveyor belt, its ceaseless revolutions powered by the magic of electricity. The hayloft too was transformed into a study in geometry, the tidy rectangles stacked like a child's puzzle, every corner meeting. Secluded from light and air, the bales helped to preserve the hay's nutrients, releasing them with a fragrant burst when their strings were cut on a midwinter day.

With the first frosts in October, haying came to an end, and, for a moment, there was a pause in the ceaseless bustle. Now there was an anniversary to celebrate. But hands accustomed to work soon fretted in idleness, and there was always leftover manure and lime to spread on fields and firewood to be delivered to customers.

As the weather cooled in earnest, Don turned his eyes to his woodlot, especially the pine trees beckoning green against the browning fields. To offset winter's drop in milk production, he had started growing Christmas trees. Starting in November, he ranged through the forest, grooming the most promising young trees. The young cattle had grazed there all summer, and the trees had a beautiful color, their boughs deep green from the rich manure.

The new year exchanged the cheer of Christmas trees for the serious business of woodcutting. From January through April, Don cut trees for firewood, pulpwood, and lumber, selling what he didn't need for himself. Beech, yellow birch, and maple were felled for firewood and left to dry until the following fall. Softwoods like fir were sent to the pulp mills in Augusta and Bucksport to meet the growing demand for paper, while white birch ended its days as toothpicks and spools.

In the muddy and unpredictable transition from winter to spring, Don switched to paperwork. As town selectman, he was responsible for doing property assessments, so April was devoted to updating the valuation book. Shirley, glad to have him inside, would work next to him, painstakingly copying the annual town records by hand. Taxes were done in May, but by then the farm was reawakening, and Don gladly returned to work outdoors, once again checking the fence line.

If the seasons passed quickly, so too did the years, and soon there were children growing alongside the farm. Their first child, Sylvia, arrived on September 30, 1952, to equal parts delight and heartbreak. Born with Down syndrome, Sylvia arrived at a time when there was little available information about her special needs and abilities. While Shirley and Don struggled to find answers, Sylvia had no such concerns. She was, in all things, unmistakably herself, and she threw herself wholeheartedly into farm life.

Four years later, labor pains sent Shirley back to the hospital in Augusta, while Don hurriedly finished the evening milking. But as Shirley awaited the arrival of her baby—and her husband!—a winter storm was raging outside. By the time Don emerged from the barn, a heavy blanket of snow had fallen, completely blocking the road. The new baby, their son Mark, was to arrive long before Don.

Now there was a family, and the warm delights of home called Don in to share dinner with his wife and children. Dinner was the biggest and heartiest meal of the day, with seasonal vegetables giving variation to the

backbone of meat and potatoes. Ham and pot roast alternated as the cen-
terpiece of the meal, with venison appearing on special occasions. Baked
beans were such a favorite that leftovers made it to the breakfast table the
next day. The traditional johnnycake was still served alongside pea soup.
And no dinner was complete without Shirley's biscuits, now eaten by the
panful. Indeed, local legend held that Don carried a ten-quart pail full of
biscuits for lunch each day.

Such family time was precious, as the march of the years competed
with the demands of each season. Sylvia, ever more determined to be
independent, followed Don around the barn, helping in any way she
could. She particularly loved feeding the cows, carefully counting as
she scooped out the correct amount of grain. Although she struggled to
maneuver the heavy wheelbarrow, she refused help, carefully pushing it
down the aisle by herself.

Mark, grown into a healthy and curious child, had already decided
that he was not a farmer. Frustrated by his own declining health, Lloyd
pressured Mark to help on the farm, but Mark had no interest in cows,
and Shirley supported her young son in his own interests. When he
struggled with reading, Shirley spent the holidays coaching him, until
the written word opened to him, sparking a lifelong interest in literacy.

With a pack of young children once again running around the farm,
Don and Lloyd were reminded of their own childhood and their frequent
trips to their grandmother's cookie jar. Laughing at the boyish hope shining in their husbands' eyes, Shirley and Marge assured their husbands
that *their* cookie jars were not bottomless, and turned instead to Edith's
famous cake recipe.

Edith's Chocolate Cake, from the *Maine Farmer*

*Cream together 1 cup sugar, ½ cup cocoa, ½ cup (scant) butter. Add 1 egg,
1 teaspoon vanilla, 1 cup sour milk. Then 1 teaspoon soda, 1 teaspoon
salt, and 1½ cups flour, sifted together. Very nice. Frost with chocolate if
you wish.*

Cookies or no cookies, the farm, with its wide sweep of open land,
was made for childhood explorations. The six cousins—Jean, Ann, Sylvia,

Beth, Peter, and Mark—were as familiar as siblings, and played and worked together from dawn until dusk. Come haying time, there were twelve extra hands to bring in the hay. Their reward came in late summer, when the barn was packed tight, and Don would arrange the bales so they could climb to the cupola. When the other children headed into the loft, disappearing in a mad scramble, Sylvia followed, equally determined if somewhat slower. Reaching the top, she gazed over the rolling hills, freed for a moment from earthbound constraints.

By 1958 Lloyd's MS had become severely debilitating, and Don took charge of the farm. Lloyd, refusing to give up, still made the daily trip to the barn, although he relied on two canes to navigate the bumpy ground. He enjoyed being around the cows, and he continued to milk as long as he could. However, although Lloyd helped as best as he was able, Don needed a farmer more than ever.

In 1960, hopefully pregnant once again, Shirley contracted hepatitis. Their boy, Dale Richard, born with great expectations, lived for only one day. His life, however short, bore a lifetime of regret; forever after they were to wonder "if he might have been the farmer." For it was becoming clear that the farm had no heir. Sylvia, passionately involved in farm life, would never be able to manage the business side, and Mark's interests led away from the farm.

Don, however, had never been one to complain. Thankful for a happy home and a thriving farm, he continued to farm carefully and steadily, never buying on credit. As a member of the Dairy Herd Improvement Association, he carefully recorded the production history of each cow, seeking to identify his best milkers. Belle and Willow, Dizzy and Queen, Pizza and Dodo—all were measured and evaluated.

A prudent farmer, Don aimed not only for high production, but, more importantly, for high returns, calculated as income over feed cost. In this he excelled, doubling his returns in ten years. Nor were his cows poor quality; his herd was often on the "honor roll," and in 1976 one of his cows received the "Iron Grandma" award, for 100,000 pounds lifetime production.

A man of community as well as family, Don, as first selectman, helped Somerville to reestablish itself as a proud and independent town, capable of self-governance. Since it had become a plantation in 1938, Somerville had been under the administration of the Department of Environmental Protection (DEP), which imposed strict zoning guidelines. Accustomed to shaping their own destiny, the local people chafed under such restrictions. Unlike the unorganized plantations in the far northern forests, Somerville was an "organized" plantation, with its own planning board, and its citizens were determined to have a voice in their future.

When the 1960s brought a flood of trailers to the area, the planning board responded with a trailer ordinance to help guide the sudden rush of development. This, they were informed by the DEP, they had no right to do. Don, seeking help from extension agents, was directed to the university, where he found a sympathetic ear in one of the professors. With expert counsel—and academic credentials—to back them up, the people of Somerville initiated a change in their legal status, and by 1970 Somerville was a full town once again.

After 162 years, much had changed in the will and ways of society, but the land was still the same. Like the five generations before him, Don worked the land, trusting it to feed his family. One man alone, he farmed more land with less labor than his forebears, the power of the tractor substituting for the shared labor of family.

Perched on the tractor's high seat, with the hum of the engine for company, there was time for reflection, as the land rolled around him. It was a type of silence, and in that stillness he wrote poetry. If he wondered about the farm's future, he did not worry. A man of the land, he was also a man of deep faith, and he saw the hand of God in the beauty around him.

In Defense of Farming

Some folks think a farmer
leads a mighty dreary life;
all they see is drudgery
and one continual strife.

They say, "You're always working,
you never travel much,
you have no time for pleasure,
to live it up, and such."

I'll admit it's not too easy,
but there is one big reward—
in the everyday experience
you have a chance to meet with God.

I meet God in the morning
just before the break of day,
and in that quiet moment
I seem to hear Him say

That He will lead and guide me,
if I will trust in Him,
through all of life's adventure
though the light sometimes be dim.

Then I see Him in the sunrise,
with the day so fresh and new,
as I look on bright green pastures
there a'sparkling in the dew.

And the cows serenely grazing,
with lush feed on every side,
seem to speak of God's great goodness,
and His promise to provide.

Then the blazing sun of noonday,
with the air so clean and good,
tells of his wondrous glory,
never fully understood.

There's a humbling effect to farming
as we wrestle with the sod:
Man can do his best at sowing
but the harvest comes from God.

Not every day's experience
goes according to our choice,
but He speaks through trial and testing,
if we're listening for His voice.

Sometimes it's been my duty
to leave home so snug and warm
to go out through woods and meadows,
facing wind and bitter storm,

While searching for an animal
that's either sick or lost,
I'm reminded of my redemption
Christ purchased at such a cost;

How he left his home in glory,
far beyond the most distant star—
how he came on Earth to suffer,
how he sought me from afar.

Then I see him in the sunset
there in the western sky,
and marvel at the splendor
He made for mortals, such as I.

And often in the evening
when the silent shadows fall,
He tells me life is fleeting—
I must be ready, should He call.

Now you may not care for farming,
but please don't pity me—
There's joy beneath the surface
the human eye can't see;

For the peace that dwells within me
no millionaire could buy—
whatever sum he'd offer
it would be vain for him to try.

There are those who have traveled widely,
here at home and some abroad,
yet in all their many journeys
they never met with God.

You can find God in the city,
or wherever you may be,
but He's nearer in the country—
that's where He deals with me.

Life, it seemed, was not too bad on a small farm in a Maine.

However, the good times of the 1970s could not last forever, and small farms across the nation were soon to feel the effect of shifting global markets. Even at the end of a dirt road in central Maine . . .

Agricultural productivity had been increasing since the 1950s, driven by advances in farm technology, but the strong markets of the 1970s had seemed capable of absorbing it all. Then secretary of agriculture Earl Butz had encouraged farmers to "plant fencerow to fencerow" and "get big or get out," and farmers had responded with record levels of production.[2]

But the 1980s were a new decade. Contracting markets suddenly transformed welcome productivity into unwelcome surplus, and heavily subsidized commodities, like grain and milk, began rapidly draining federal coffers.[3] The government struggled to find an appropriate policy response, and in a strange twist, the agricultural department began to pay farmers *not* to produce. As price followed demand downward, farmers fought desperately, and often futilely, to survive. Thousands of farms succumbed to the national Farm Crisis, and rural communities declined.[4]

Don, a longtime member of the Agricultural Stabilization and Conservation Service (ASCS), was well informed of the national situation, and he knew the USDA was seeking to decrease milk production. In 1986, he learned of the Dairy Herd Buyout Program. In return for terminating their herd, farmers would receive compensation payments for several years, determined by their historic production level.[5]

Reluctantly, Don considered his options. In a strange way it seemed fortuitous. He had recently been diagnosed with prostate cancer, and he wondered if the twice-daily milking would soon be more than he could handle. There was no eager child to take up the reins, and yet he still needed to support his family. Trusting in fate, he submitted his bid, not expecting it to be accepted.

To his surprise, his bid was approved, and the slow process of closing the dairy began. His herd, so carefully selected for improved dairy genetics, was destined for the slaughterhouse. Over the next few months, the barn gradually emptied.

That winter, without morning and evening milking to attend to, Don delved more deeply into his woodlot, grooming the finest Christmas trees and selling pulpwood and timber. In the summer, when the grass, ungrazed, stretched high, a local farmer asked Don if he could rent some of the pasture for his heifers. The remaining fields still made good hay, and Don faithfully fertilized his fields, selling the richness of his land to eager buyers.

In 1994, at the age of seventy-two, Don sold the farm and most of the land. He kept only forty acres, a mixture of fields and forest. There, on a hilltop overlooking the farm, he built himself and Shirley a small, neat house, simple and easy to care for.

After 186 years, there was no young farmer waiting to assume the care of the land.

Farming, it seemed, had become a historical occupation in Somerville, Maine. Of the ninety-six farms that had filled the plates of Somerville families in 1880, only one remained. On Hewett Road, the barn was quiet and the fields were empty. Only the sound of one old tractor stirred the morning air, because for Don, there was still work to do. A Maine house still needs firewood, and stone walls still need clearing . . .

NOTES

1. http://www.antiquefarming.com/johndeeregp.html, March 23, 2013.

2. Iowa Public Television, *The Farm Crisis*. Online text of video, posted September 6, 2013. Accessed April 28, 2014, http://www.iptv.org/iowastories/story.cfm/farm-crisis/10632/frc_20130701/video.

3. University of California, Berkeley, "The Economics of the US Dairy Program," online lecture notes for Course EEP141, Fall 2007. Accessed online on April 28, 2014, http://are.berkeley.edu/courses/EEP141/fall2007/lecture_notes/Dairy-Program.pdf.

4. Iowa Public Television, *The Farm Crisis*.

5. University of California, Berkeley, "The Economics of the US Dairy Program."

AUGUST 2010

POTATOES

MID-AUGUST and undeniably midsummer, but, pulling up the shade, I can see that the potatoes have already ripened, their stems brown and withered. Given the shortness of our summer, we have selected early-maturing varieties, but even so I am surprised by the speed of things. Still, we will not harvest them yet; I will leave them in the ground a few more weeks, allowing their skins to thicken for storage.

Patience, however, is too hard a crop for my father. One evening I hear his voice in the garden and look out to see Anil digging in the potato bed, my father on one side, Keiran on the other. This is a new harvest for both grandfather and grandson, and they are equally rapt, peering intently into the dirt. When my father comes inside, his face is shining, part curious scientist, part eager child.

"I've never dug potatoes before," he says, holding out the tubers in his large, strong hands. "Now I just need to see the planting in the spring . . ."

A week later, Anil and I head out to harvest in earnest. Keiran, now an experienced potato digger, is close beside us, shovel in hand. Born with an insatiable desire to dig, he follows us down the row, burying his shovel deep in the earth, then watching the dirt slide off. Our cat, Diego, likewise a natural digger, peers curiously into the emerging holes. A careless toss bestows an unexpected benediction of soil on his white back, and he dashes off, his colors momentarily blurred.

When Keiran eventually catches up with me, he notices the potatoes rising from the soil and the sudden flash of golden skin. Excited, he runs to retrieve them, lifting them out of the dark soil triumphantly. Considering what to do with his catch, he looks first in the bucket, but the wagon has a larger pile, and he drops them in with an audible thud. "Gently," I urge him. "We will eat them all winter."

Excitement, however, outweighs restraint, so Anil sits Sarita in the row while he supervises the handling of Keiran's harvest.

With Keiran's "help" we work more slowly, and the sky darkens as we hurry to pull the last of the Yukon Golds. We have planted twice as many Yukons to compensate for their relatively low yield, willing to sacrifice space for their rich flavor. However, it turns out to be little sacrifice: From five pounds of seed potatoes, we harvest forty-seven pounds of edible tubers. Even with lower yields, it is easy to see why settlers planted potatoes in their first clearing, relying on them to carry the household through the winter. Our own basement is cool already, and as we spread them out on newspaper, their golden skin shines through their dusty jackets, promising a rich reward.

A few weeks pass before we can harvest the rest, but Keiran's excitement only increases. With the Yukons harvested, we turn to the rows of All Blue, wondering what we will find. At planting, we had high hopes, but the potato beetles apparently shared our preference. Despite our best deterrents, it was their favored variety, and the plants had withered under the beetle's unrelenting assault. The potatoes, conceived in hope, have stayed small, and plant after plant yields golf-ball-size tubers, their skins pockmarked.

After the besieged Blues, it is a relief to turn to Sangre, a large red-skinned variety. Excited to have a larger quarry, Keiran follows my fork eagerly, calling us repeatedly to admire his catch. Then, lifting my fork, I feel a *really* large one, large even to me, and it is my turn to shout in excitement. Descending into the dirt, Keiran tries to dig it out, but it is too large for one hand. "Holy moly!" he exclaims. "Holy moly potato!" and I laugh in delighted agreement as he holds it aloft, two-handed above his head.

We finish one row, then another, until dusk sends Anil and Sarita in to start dinner. Turning to check on Keiran, I realize his enthusiastic digging has devolved into a crawl down the row.

"Do you want to go inside?" I ask, but he shakes his head immediately, desperate, as always, to stay outside. Like a small burrowing animal, he claims the hole I have just vacated, settling deep inside. He is usually hesitant to lie on the ground, spurning even the soft grass, and I watch in surprise as he leans back into the soft dirt, lifting his face to the sky.

Following me on hands and knees, he moves from hole to hole, shaping each to fit his body. I have never seen him so comfortably close to the earth, his pants covered in dirt. Straightening up at the end of the row, I see him on his belly, inching his way along the ground.

"Are you a worm?" I ask him, laughing, and he smiles up at me, pleased to be recognized.

As we brush mud off boots and body, I look up to see a patch of a rainbow hanging above the barn. The colors are bright, each stripe distinct, but it is a fragment only, each end dissolving into air. I pick Keiran up, standing him on the fence so he can see over the tall weeds. He stares, fascinated, then turns his head, searching for the rest.

Spying the cat, he calls to him enthusiastically. "Come on, Diego— come see the rainbow!"

I laugh, hugging my sweet boy, but, perhaps responding to the invitation in his voice, Diego jumps up beside us. Together we watch for a few moments more, until the rainbow suddenly dissolves, and we are staring at clear sky.

Returned to normal delights, we remember dinner waiting inside. As we open the door, the rich smell of roasting potatoes rushes out to greet us, the combined love of farm and family, welcoming, sustaining.

Rainbow Roasted Potatoes

Gather an assortment of colored potatoes, skins intact. For the best flavor, select freshly harvested heirloom varieties, available in your garden or farmers' market. Preheat oven to 400 degrees. Wash potatoes, then dice into 1-inch cubes. Toss with enough olive oil to gently coat, and sprinkle with kosher salt. Spread on a large baking sheet and roast in oven until crispy on the outside and soft in the center, turning every 10 to 15 minutes to brown all sides.

August 2010

Land

LATE AUGUST, only a month since the tractor arrived, but already it is an integral part of our lives. Pastures have been cut, pens are cleaned, and a neatly mown path stretches down to the brook. Even the road is marked by the tractor's passage, the soft dirt imprinted with the tracks of its heavy wheels.

Stepping out of the house, Keiran is drawn irresistibly along its path, running full tilt, delighted to follow the tractor's trail. Encouraged by all we have accomplished, we have decided to take a family excursion to the back field—a minor expedition with a baby in tow—and so we emerge, one, two, three, and four, saddled like a desert caravan. Keiran, now a proud big brother, races ahead of us like an exuberant puppy.

Spying Don's truck parked along the road, Keiran clambers up the bank, calling for his friend. Don, shirtless, straddles the stone wall, clearing away the encroaching brush. It is an act of love and pride, this careful tending of property lines, and he is oblivious to our presence on the road.

Keiran, however, demands attention, arriving like an insistent bee in front of him. Straightening, Don spies us and waves, carefully picking his way down through the rocks. Keiran darts alongside, a hummingbird beside a heron, the two ends of human motion.

When he reaches us, Don laughs at his own efforts.

"I like to see across the fields," he says, "but they have already grown up so much." Ruefully he adds, "It will probably be the last time I do it." Having sold his mower, he cannot cut enough by hand to clear the view. Bent perhaps a bit more, he returns to his work, Keiran running glad escort beside him.

Anil and I turn into the field, but it is not long before I hear Keiran's feet running behind me. He arrives with outstretched hand showcasing his latest apple. The fruit has grown rapidly in the summer heat, and it almost fills his hand. I remind him how small they used to be, and he looks, evaluating, then asks, "Getting bigger and bigger?"

He has come to understand the world in relation to the farm, the passage of time defined by the arrival, and departure, of each season's delights. A few nights before, surveying his dinner, he had asked—hopefully—for peas.

"The peas have gone by," I reminded him. "We won't have more until next year."

After considering this, he looked at me. "Snow coming?" he asked, and so we explained that snow would return with the winter and the early dark.

Hopeful again, he looked up. "See the moon?" he asked, his eyes shining with undimmed memory.

Surprised, I laughed. All summer, with the sun lingering in the sky, the moon had been an infrequent and pallid visitor, and I had assumed he had forgotten his old friend. Now, looking into his bright eyes, I saw the moon reflected there.

Still, moon and snow and even peas are for the future, and, with no shortage of present delights, he heads for the blackberry patch. The canes tower above his head, their glistening fruits held high, but he is both determined and realistic. Carefully, he searches until he finds a leaning cane, its dark treasures within easy reach. Free to help himself, he eats the berries by the fistful, grunting like a small bear, his cheeks stained purple-black. Knowing the briefness of such seasonal delights, Anil indulges him, bending the tallest canes down to Keiran's level.

While the boys linger, feasting, Sarita and I stroll, enjoying a rare moment alone. Beneath her hat, her eyes are wide, and she watches me intently, as if I contained the whole world. She has changed in the past few weeks, emerged, and her eyes shine with joy and intelligence and humor, as if she were sharing a secret. She smiles—her inimitable slow smile of delight—and I smile back, our communication unhindered by silence.

Keiran, momentarily sated, rejoins us in a rush, eager to lead the parade. Although it was impossible to ignore the berries, the main attraction lay across the brook: Two tractors, big green and little blue, beckoned from the back field. Neil Peaslee had started haying our fields, and he had told Keiran, with a wink and a smile, that he could "drive" the tractors whenever they were idle. Keiran had been desperate to try them out, and now, goal in sight, he races ahead of us.

Summer, however, has many charms, and the bright yellow petals of a black-eyed Susan interrupt his progress. Wading into the field, he bends their hairy stems, but their fibers are strong, resisting separation. With a gentle hand, I show him how to twist rather than bend the stalks, until their fibers reluctantly part. Triumphant, he carries the flowers in a careful bouquet, their yellow heads nodding in time with his yellow boots.

Down the field and across the river he leads us, his boots well able to ford the small trickle of summer. Ascending the other side, a small rise obscures his view of the tractors, and he cries out in disappointment.

"Let's go over the mountain," I tell him, "and see what we can see."

Confused by the tractors' sudden disappearance, he nevertheless plods up hopefully, his faith in me limitless.

Halfway up, the tractors reappear, and with a shout, he runs the final steps over the hill. He is still too short to climb onto the step, but he waits beneath it, bouncing, until we reach him. With a whoop and a swing, Anil boosts him onto the big John Deere, and he stands, his head barely visible over the wheel, happily driving.

Sarita, still immune to tractors' charms, makes her own desires known, so I climb onto the smaller blue Ford in search of a comfortable seat. As she settles down to nurse, I am free to look back across the fields, to our house and barn and grazing goats. We are only partway up the field, but already the sky is huge, the land rolling around me. Against the brilliant green grass, the white Saanens shine like small fragments of cloud come to earth.

Closer at hand, Keiran spins his tractor's steering wheel in gleeful delight. "Going too fast" he repeats, over and over, thrilling to the imagined power of his machine.

There can be no rushing such delights, but eventually we lure Keiran away from the tractors for the final ascent to the back field. It is hot and bright in the freshly mown grass, so we follow the forest's edge, grateful for its quiet coolness. Sarita's dark eyes open wide in the shade, peering into the shadowy forest, and Keiran breathes more easily, his sturdy young legs still small for such a hike. Nearing the top, we climb out into the sun again, seeking the highest ground.

Standing together on the crest of the hill, we can see in all directions, our farm joined to a greater whole. From here, it is easy to imagine the land the settlers found, for the forest stretches out on all sides, engulfing the surrounding hills. The farm's cleared land dips below us in a smooth bowl, scooped out of the forest, but the trees wait, ever hopeful, casting their seeds into the fields' edges.

Left to her own devices, nature would return our fields to forest, and so we have tended them carefully, gratefully aware of the generations that have shaped this land with love and hope and enduring labor. But nature is a generous mother, smiling on her children's play. She has not treated our efforts with spite, but instead has blessed our toil with her fertility, feeding us from her bounty.

Lifted so close to the sky, I exult, but I also fear for the future of our farm and the surrounding land. Since the settlers first arrived, this land has been logged, providing a livelihood to many families. The forest has always provided a rich resource, but for the first time, I feel worried.

For the past month, I've awoken to the sound of chainsaws, felling the trees that top our ridge. As I've watched the clearing expand, I've grown more afraid for us, and the land. The forest has supported our farm, grounding it in the larger ecosystem. To the north, the forest covers two long ridges, sheltering the rich valley where the brook runs. At the end of the valley, Patrick Mountain rises gently, a small destination of hope and completion.

Now they are clear-cutting, and I feel helpless and scared. Will new developments top our ridge, large houses commanding the view? Will the marsh and brook, already fragile, be swallowed up by development? For the first time, I feel land-hungry, frustrated by my lack of control over this area's future. This has always been a special place, and I long to conserve it.

As for the future of our own farm, more questions than answers still remain. Will this be only a historical farm of six generations, or can we restore it as a living, breathing, *viable* family farm? Will we be able to reestablish the farm as a commercial venture and fulfill our goal of making it a community resource, enabling others to experience small-farm life?

So far, our survival has been in large part because we *are* a family farm, in many and unexpected ways. Not only has the farm drawn our family together, its long tendrils reaching across state and national boundaries, but it has also inspired commitment across generations. Despite their concerns about the farm's economic rewards, my parents have no doubts about the value of life on a farm, with its deep connections to land and community. Their repeated generosity has enabled us to make several key investments, keeping our dream a possibility.

Together, we are looking toward the future, embodied in Keiran's delighted dance on the hilltop. It has been a long time since we've walked so far with him, and he revels in his high perch, lifted close to the sky. Below us, the land spreads out, open to our curious eyes. Our home, so familiar, is suddenly only part of a larger canvas, the goats no more than small dots.

"Do you see the barn?" we ask Keiran, wondering how much he recognizes.

"Right there," he answers immediately, his small finger reaching into the distance.

On our return, though, Keiran bypasses the house, heading instead toward Don's tractor shed. Even the brightness of the Kubota has not obscured the deeper enchantment of the old John Deere. His small body dwarfed by the tall wheels, Keiran begs for five minutes at the wheel.

As we settle him on the tractor, he sings, overjoyed, "Many long years ago . . ." Perched atop his mythic beast, he spins the steering wheel back and forth, revving enthusiastically.

There is only the one tractor in the shed now, and it looks strangely empty without its stall mate. Although Don had hoped to sell his other tractor to an antiques dealer, necessity had forced his hand, and he had sold it to the highest bidder. It seemed a cruel separation, yet Don appeared more resigned than my own small son, who protests loudly when we finally pull him off.

"Bye-bye, John Deere! See you tomorrow," he calls back, blissfully confident in his own future, here on the farm he loves so well.

EPILOGUE

WE CANNOT all live on small farms—nor do we all want to—but the *experience* of life on a small farm should be available to all. In our high-tech world, it is vital that our children also have high-nature experiences. How can they know that the world is not defined by the screen if they don't dig into the ground or look up into limitless sky?

If our children are truly to understand their great gift of life, they must know that birth and death are more than virtual. Surrounded by both on a farm, we know what it is to live and therefore to die. The small seed—buried in the dirt and swollen with water—bursts with life in a miracle small only in size. Watching the sprout emerge, stretching to the sun, our children *experience* vitality, the power to grow with vigor and meaning. Like the sweet gift of sap in the spring, we feel life coursing through our veins and know that we are alive. Should we not also burst with life, exuberant in our passage, reaching for the sun?

Next to the bursting seed, there is also the reality of decay, as death feeds new life. Climbing into the loft, we feel the scratchy prickles of hay against our softer skin. The grasses, cut in their ripe fullness, are slowly drying, dying, to become the feast of winter. Here among the bales are noisy tunnels of play, later transformed into a quiet fortress of solitude.

On a farm we learn the responsibility of daily chores—that life, in our care, rushes hungrily toward us, demanding food and drink. Here, too, we learn that pursuit does not gain all, that we must be quiet and still if we are to earn a young animal's trust. If we learn, we receive the reward for patience: a moment of connection, a nose cool on our hand, and a softly exhaled breath.

We must ensure that there are still small farms, for the health of our children is intertwined with their future. As farms disappear, from 40 percent of US households in 1900 to 1.8 percent in 2012, fewer children have direct family connections to farms.[1] Increasingly, we must find *new* ways to get our children on a farm—for an afternoon, a week, a semester. In Norway, they are doing it already, developing over two hundred cooperative programs between farms and schools in the past fifteen years.[2]

We are an incredibly innovative species, creators of an amazing technological world; let's use those skills to reengage with the natural and reconnect farms and children by sending them to farms after school, for summer camps, or for their junior year.

Let us write our own story, for the choices are ours. Although *we* must end, let each individual story be just one chapter. Let us choose to live with awareness and appreciation for our moment in the sun. Let the land continue to nurture, as she has always nurtured. Let us not drown her out, but join our voices with hers, each granted a stanza in her endless song.

Best of all, let us bring our children, for their high, young voices swoop and lilt with her laughter, the sweetest melody of all. Walk with them to the end of the road, where it is quiet enough to hear the land. Our voices are clearer there, just one voice among many: goats calling, hawk screaming, children laughing, tractor rumbling.

When our voices fade, the land will still be there, singing.

NOTES

1. Louv, *Last Child in the Woods*. Updated with the 2010 federal population data of 116.7 million households and the 2012 agricultural census data of 2.1 million farm households.

2. Linda Jolly and Erling Krogh, *School Farm Cooperation in Norway: Background and Recent Research* (2010). For an inspiring video example, see http://www.youtube.com/watch?v=xpwIb9on-Gk.

APPENDIX A

FURTHER READING

THE FOLLOWING books provide a glimpse of the *experience* of farming in Maine over the years. They are a combination of fiction, nonfiction, poetry, and photography. What they share is their ability to provide a window into a different time and place. How much poorer we are when we lose our understanding of our past, and yet, sadly, many of these books are almost forgotten.

The books are arranged chronologically, by the year of their setting.

1. *Come Spring* by Ben Ames Williams. Fiction, first published in 1940. Available since 2000 through the Union, Maine Historical Society, 343 Common Rd., Union, ME 04862. http:///unionhistoricalsociety.org. The book follows the (historical) Robbins family from their first arrival in Maine in 1776 through their next eight years, as they struggle to create, and survive on, a family farm. Williams says it best himself, in his introduction:

> *The attempt in this book has been to tell the story of the founding of a small Maine town, by ordinary people, in what was then an ordinary way. It was the way in which towns were founded from the Atlantic*

seaboard west to the great plains, by stripping off the forest and putting the land to work . . . People like them made this country, and towns like this one were and are the soil in which this country's roots are grounded.

2. *A Day's Work: A Sampler of Historic Maine Photographs 1860–1920, Parts I and II.* Compiled and annotated by William Bunting and published in 1997. Available through Tilbury House, 12 Starr St., Thomaston, ME 04861. www.tilburyhouse.com. Bunting's books provide a photographic account of Maine life during the end of the "pre-petroleum economy." Although the photos are fascinating, it is Bunting's annotations that draw the reader into the scene, with all the detail and humor of a local Yankee guide. Regarding the rise, and fall, of Maine's famous stone walls, Bunting writes:

The Book of Job was doubtless well thumbed by many a sore thumb in countless humble Maine capes. Well before the last humpbacked old wall builder had claimed his just reward, the forest had begun reclaiming the hard-won land. Soon, thousands of miles served only to organize millions of acres of trees. Later New Englanders were at a loss to explain what had gotten into their wall-building forefathers, although some suspected it had been rum, by the barrel.

3. *As the Earth Turns* by Gladys Hasty Carroll. Fiction, published in 1933. Available through Blackberry Books, 617 East Neck Rd., Nobleboro, ME 04555. chimfarm@gwi.net. The book follows the Shaw family farm through one year in 1930, while the various members struggle to adapt to the changing world. Depicts the joys and conflicts of rural life at that time. As Denise Pendleton writes in her introduction:

America was . . . still reeling from the pace of rapid modernization and social change that had set in at the turn of the century . . . In rural Maine, life balanced precariously between the old and the new in 1930 . . . Even if they stayed in the country, which fewer and fewer did, they would soon cease to be entirely of the country. Ultimately, [the book] is a celebration of the rural, but its story, by its careful attention to the details of rural life, captures the conflicts inherent to such a life in a modern world.

4. *Northern Farm* by Henry Beston. Nonfiction, published in 1948. Available through Blackberry Books, 617 East Neck Rd., Nobleboro, ME 04555. chimfarm@gwi.net. Set in 1931, the same time period as *As the Earth Turns,* this book chronicles the author's conscious decision to forgo modern conveniences for the slower, deeper connection of country life. Describing in poetic detail one year of farm life, it raises questions that are still pertinent today. As Beston writes:

> *When the nineteenth century and the industrial era took over our western civilization, why was it that none of us saw that we should all presently become peoples without a past? Yet this is precisely what has happened . . .*
>
> *I do not feel so bewildered when I return to my own fields. The country cannot avoid being a part of its own era . . . yet we are not without a past and never shall be. For us the furrow is the furrow since the beginning of the world, and the plough handles are to our hands what they were to those who cleared the land.*

5. *Balance: A Late Pastoral* by Russell Libby. Poems, published in 2007. Available through Blackberry Books, 617 East Neck Rd., Nobleboro, ME 04555. chimfarm@gwi.net. Russell, best known as the executive director of the Maine Organic Farmers and Gardeners Association, epitomized the best of Maine's new generation of farmers, who re-valued traditional small-scale agriculture as a way to sustainably meet the needs of the future.

As Russell says in his poem, "Balance":

Forest on one side, fields on the other;
stone walls are the fulcrum.
If we weigh the history of this farm,
the scales have tilted towards trees.

I shouldn't be surprised.
These fields all began as forest . . .

6. *From the Land: Maine Farms at Work.* Photographs by Bridget Besaw, text by John Piotti. Nonfiction, published June 8, 2010. Available through Maine Farmland Trust, 97 Main St., Belfast, ME 04915. www

.mainfarmlandtrust.org. A beautiful and hopeful glimpse into the future of small family farms in Maine. John Piotti writes:

> *Farming in Maine defies any single label. It is at once robust, thriving, threatened, modern, ancient, venerable, dirty, tedious, and hip.*

The book profiles seven of these farms, who have embraced the experience of farming. As Philip Retberg from Quill's End Farm states:

> *Every year our children get to see real life—birth, life, and death. These are things that we've been trying to shield our society from for fifty years. Farm kids get joy and heartbreak and reality wrapped into every season.*

"THE RHODORA"

BY RALPH WALDO EMERSON

ON BEING ASKED, WHENCE IS THE FLOWER?

In May, when sea-winds pierced our solitudes,
I found the fresh Rhodora in the woods,
Spreading its leafless blooms in a damp nook,
To please the desert and the sluggish brook.
The purple petals, fallen in the pool,
Made the black water with their beauty gay;
Here might the red-bird come his plumes to cool,
And court the flower that cheapens his array.
Rhodora! if the sages ask thee why
This charm is wasted on the earth and sky,
Tell them, dear, that if eyes were made for seeing,
Then Beauty is its own excuse for being:
Why thou wert there, O rival of the rose!
I never thought to ask, I never knew:
But, in my simple ignorance, suppose
The self-same Power that brought me there brought you.